FROM PITCH TO PRINT

THE NONFICTION WRITER'S 10-STEP PLAN TO GETTING PUBLISHED

DR. JENNIFER DORSEY

broad
book
press

T0286152

Broad Book Press, Publisher

Cover and interior design by Andrew Welyczko, AbandonedWest Creative, Inc.

Paperback ISBN: 9798985191332
eBook ISBN: 9798985191349

Published in the United States by Broad Book Press, an imprint of Broad Book Group, Edwardsville, IL.

Library of Congress Control Number: 2024902955

CONTENTS

INTRODUCTION

I LOVE BOOKS. PERIOD. I love everything about them. I love everything about making them. Don't you just love the smell of a new book? When you crack open that spine, you smell the ink, and you touch the paper. It's a true feeling of joy to open a new book. That's how I feel every time I start a new book project too. I love the sense of possibility, and the realization that creating something new, fresh, and different is right there at my fingertips.

For those of us who work in book publishing, that sense of awe and wonder never really goes away. This is an incredibly unique and interesting business, but it does have its challenges. Over the last 25-plus years I have worked with authors across the world in all kinds of topic areas. Nonfiction is my specialty, so I have seen everything from books about car maintenance and repair to leadership and crafts. Working in the nonfiction space has allowed me to work with some of the world's most interesting and unique subject matter experts. But no matter who I work with—and I have worked with all kinds of people—I always get the same question: How does a book get published?

The answer to that question is somewhat complicated. The process for publishing a fiction book is quite different from that of publishing a nonfiction book. So, while I can't speak to the fiction side of the business, I do have some insight into how the nonfiction publishing world works after 25 years in the business. And the biggest lesson I have learned in that time is that there is a serious need for democratization of information when it comes to the publishing process. By that, I mean that there is simply no value in keeping potential authors in the dark about what to expect in the publishing process. I always find it intriguing that some people want to gatekeep this information, because it serves us all well to work with authors who are educated in the systems that make publishing work.

Over the years, as our industry has moved away from purely traditional publishing models and started to consider other means of publishing as viable options, information has been shared more widely than in the past. Now, authors have many options available to them when it comes to choosing a publishing journey. Self-publishing is currently experiencing a renaissance, allowing authors to have more creative control while still producing a highly commercial product. Hybrid publishing is now a much more well-oiled machine than it used to be, allowing authors and publishers to work together as equal partners in the business of publishing a book. Traditional publishing is also moving into a period of change as the financial ramifications of an ever-evolving content landscape change the game and the value of print and digital publishing.

This is an exciting time to be a nonfiction author.

WHY THIS BOOK

I wanted to write about how you can take your book from concept to publication because I have seen many nonfiction authors struggle over the years with what they didn't know. And you don't know what you don't know until you're in the weeds. This book isn't an exhaustive, encyclopedic look at everything that you need to know about publishing. Rather, it is the first-timer's survey course into the process of growing your idea into a fully fledged book project. My goal is to provide you with an insider's perspective on what works and what doesn't as you make decisions about your publishing path. And hopefully educating you about some of the eccentricities of the book business along the way. By the time you finish this book, you should have a better understanding of how the pitch, proposal, negotiation, and launch processes work. In other words, my goal is to give you enough information to be dangerous.

WHAT TO EXPECT IN THIS BOOK

This book is broken up into 10 steps. The initial steps are assessment based. In other words, they are designed to help you flesh out your idea so that you have a firm grasp of what it is that you plan to pitch. Then, we move on to more prescriptive chapters in which you will not only write a pitch, but craft a full proposal as well. Finally, you'll notice that I weave in conversations throughout the book about choosing a particular publishing path. We'll delve into some of the highlights of self-publishing, hybrid publishing, and traditional publishing, so you can take stock of what it is you want from this process and choose the path that is right for you.

Each step includes an activity. I encourage you to take pauses between each step so that you can complete the activity, as each one will scaffold the material you need to create a strong pitch and proposal. If you do not plan to go the traditional publishing route, and instead wish to self-publish or work with a book packager, these steps are still important for you. Why? Because if you are planning to self-publish, then you are acting as the publisher for your book. And that means your book is your business. Think of the groundwork you lay here as the basis for a business plan for your book. Even if you never pitch it traditionally, it's important to have all of your pieces together so you have confidence about the project you are publishing.

I hope you have fun with this process. I absolutely love taking a book from concept to print. There is nothing more gratifying than seeing what started out as the nugget of an idea turn into a real-life book. Some days, you feel like you will never get there, and that the project is just a dud. Every writer feels that way. In fact, editors feel that way a lot of the time too. But I encourage you to take heart, put in the work, and believe in your project. I promise you: the time and the work you put into crafting a project and choosing a publishing path will be so worth it when you see your name on the cover of that book. Let's get started!

STEP 1

Interview Yourself

LET'S TALK ABOUT your book idea and how you relate to it as the author. That's where every book starts anyway—with an idea or a concept. But what distinguishes a commercially viable book from a pet project starts with you and where you fit into the marketplace of ideas. What does that mean? Well, the marketplace of ideas is exactly what it sounds like: It's where we buy and sell our ideas and intellectual property.

Think of it like this: Every product you see and every service you use from cars and baby wipes to oil changes and legal representation has been birthed thanks to someone having an idea and executing on it. Your book is no different. It is **your** product (or service, depending on how you view your message). Many people have a really great idea in their head, but is it a book? Is it something that people are going to spend their hard-earned money on at the cash register? Will they say, "Yes! I want this book," whether it's being priced at $20 or $45 or even $50 or $75?

The answer lies in you. What will set you apart in this content-driven media environment is leaning into your role as a subject-matter expert. In this chapter, you will start to think of yourself in that way: as an expert in your field or topic area. And what's the best way to learn more about an expert? Interview them—which is what you're going to do with yourself in this chapter.

ARE YOU THE RIGHT PERSON TO WRITE A BOOK?

When you go to the nonfiction shelf at your local bookstore, what kind of books catch your eye? Beyond looking at covers, what's one of the first things you probably look for? A qualified author. You wouldn't buy a book about investing that is written by someone who is known for being an incredible baker, would you? Likewise, you probably wouldn't peruse the cooking section thinking, "If only there was a book about desserts by a well-known financier!" No, you would buy the investing book written by a certified financial planner or known investment broker. You would buy the dessert book written by a qualified pastry chef.

Your qualifications matter. If you are taking the journey of nonfiction authorship, you must have a personal stake in your subject matter that goes beyond pure interest. Do you remember the Rhetorical Triangle from your college composition class? (Thanks, Aristotle!) Ethos, pathos, and logos are the three kinds of arguments you can make in an essay. Ethos involves a writer or speaker's qualifications as a subject-matter expert. That's what you should analyze when thinking about why you are the right person to write your book. What qualifies you as an expert on your topic, whether that be personal or professional experience, is your ethos. It's what makes readers look at your author biography on the back cover and think, "Yes! This person knows their stuff. I'm buying their book."

This is the first time brainstorming is going to be a really big part of your process. Let's say that you have your strong idea, and you think it should be a book. That's great! Now, ask yourself if you are the right subject matter expert for this book. Think of all of the ways that you are that expert, brainstorm it, and write them all down. Think of all the ways that you already are out there in the marketplace of ideas with your content or your professional life and do a little bit of brainstorming about how you as an expert can be a part of that overall ecosystem of content.

I hate to tell you this, but you can't just write a book because something interests you and expect people to buy it. You have to be connected to your topic in some valuable way. It's non-negotiable that you need to be a subject matter expert, or you need to already write about that topic. It's vital that you have that connection. For example, I can't say, "I like hot air balloons so I'm going to write a book about hot air balloons. I don't even own a hot air balloon, nor have I ever seen one in person. I just think they're cool, so I'll write a book about them." Stop. Nope. You can enjoy hot air balloons all you like, but you're not the right person to write a book about hot air balloons if you don't own and operate one. Know who you are in relation to your topic and be able to explain that to your reader.

Enthusiasm counts here, too. In other words, be excited about your topic! Editors, agents, salespeople, and book consumers can see your passion throughout the life of a book, from the pitching process to your marketing outreach. Your enthusiasm about your topic endears you to your chosen audience and stakeholders. So, ask yourself what your level of enthusiasm is about your topic. And, while that enthusiasm helps build and keep your audience, it's also an essential element here because you should actually enjoy yourself as an author! Why write about something if you're not feeling the love for your topic?

One way you can get that enthusiasm across, especially to editors and agents, is to first be clear about your concept. Have it nailed down and be able to talk about it succinctly. You're the expert, remember? So, own it. Second, know how to get someone else excited and interested in your topic. It starts with you, how you write about your topic, and how you speak about it to others. If you are pitching to agents and editors, that means you use an engaging hook and write a compelling query letter (more on that later). If you are going the custom publication route, it means you use that hook as your primary selling point to customers. But you can't create that engaging hook until you have a clear book idea origin story.

WHAT IS YOUR BOOK IDEA ORIGIN STORY?

I always like to tell people that every book idea has an origin story, just like a superhero. Your idea didn't just magically pop into your head— you thought of it over time. Maybe you cultivated it in in ways that you haven't even thought of yet. To really tell a relevant story to an editor or to an agent about your book, you have to think a little bit about that origin story: Where did your idea come from?

Let's talk a little bit about how you can determine your idea's origin story. First, you need to have a noticeably clear concept in mind when you are writing a nonfiction book that helps it (and you) stand out from the crowd. And that concept came from somewhere in your world. Your book idea could have come from:

- Personal lived experience
- Historical events that you have been a part of
- Your relationship with a unique or notable person, place, or thing
- Unusual life circumstances
- Your job or business
- A hobby in which you have specific expertise
- Academia
- Travel
- A once-in-a-lifetime event
- Religious influence

Once you've pinpointed the catalytic environment that sparked your book idea, think about how you shaped that kernel of an idea into the full book concept. Ask yourself:

- what kind of research you did to determine your concept's viability as a book;
- how you built the concept's structure for the book;
- who helped you along the way (other experts, researchers, colleagues, friends, family).

Don't worry if your book is not written yet. All of these questions can easily be answered at the initial stages of your publishing journey. For now, you simply want to be able to expound the how and why of your book in terms of how it started in your mind.

IS YOUR BRAND BOOK-READY?

Yes, you are a brand—especially in the marketplace of ideas. As a subject-matter expert, you are (or at least you should be) deeply involved in the ecosystem surrounding your book's topic. Perhaps you've been working on your book idea for a long time, or it's an idea that has been swimming in your head for years. Even if it's been sitting in a drawer, and you just haven't quite known what to do with it, you have probably been working in your topic area for some time. For example, maybe it's a topic that you've been doing speaking engagements about, or you've been attending events and talking to people about it. Maybe it's a part of your everyday business. Maybe it's a class that you teach. Perhaps it's a hobby that you have a level of expertise in like crafting, baking, or travel. Book ideas can come from all kinds of places (remember your book's origin story). Anytime you have something that resonates with people in an area of your professional or personal life, whether it's in person or whether it's online, it might be a viable concept for a book project. Think about what your book dream looks like in relation to your personal brand. The two will ultimately be dovetailed together when you start to pitch your book to agents, editors, or readers themselves.

Marketing plays a huge role in your personal brand as it relates to your book. For example, how do you plan to market this book? Gone are the days when book publishers take over and say, "Sit back, relax, and let us sell your book." The publishing boom of the 1990s and early 2000s is history. That's not the world that we live in anymore. We live in a very high-touch world where authors are in constant communication with their audiences whether that's on social media, via e-mail lists or websites, or with speaking engagements, courses, and masterminds. So, you need to get in brainstorming mode to think about all the ways that you can help sell that book.

Here's how to tell if your personal brand is book-ready:

- You have the subject-matter street cred to write about your topic.
- You are actively involved in work and/or organizations that support your topic.

- You produce other content about your topic—like blog posts, articles, or interviews.
- You show others how to engage with your topic through educational outreach like courses, webinars, or workshops.
- You speak about your topic at professional events and conferences.
- You have a professional social media following.
- You have or prepared to create a professional website for yourself and your topic.
- You have a newsletter and subscriber list.

Now, not all of these branding elements may apply to you. For example, if you are a historian writing a new book about the history of NASA spouses, you may not be leading masterminds. That's okay! It's not applicable to you. But are you speaking to historical societies or writing compelling articles about your topic? Then that applies to you. Feel free to tinker with this list to fit your own branding needs as you complete **Activity 1: Write Your Author Bio.**

In the next chapter, we'll talk about the viability of your book idea.

Activity 1
WRITE YOUR AUTHOR BIO

Use this worksheet to begin drafting your author bio based on the questions you've tackled in this chapter. This is your opportunity to introduce yourself to agents, editors, and readers, so don't be shy! You will use your author bio in several ways during your publishing journey from your professional social media accounts and website to your book proposal and—eventually—the back cover of your book.

1. Credentials

....

....

....

....

....

....

2. Connection to the topic

....

....

....

....

....

....

3. Professional affiliations

....

....

....

....

....

....

4. Endorsements

....
....
....
....
....
....

5. Personal information

....
....
....
....
....
....
....

6. Additional information

....
....
....
....
....
....
....
....
....
....
....
....
....
....
....
....

Determine Your Book Idea's Viability

NOW THAT YOU HAVE spent some time interviewing yourself and thinking about who you are as an author, it's time to think a little more deeply about your book topic. To do that, it's important to think about how your book will perform in the marketplace of ideas. Keep in mind that, for most writers, a book is a labor of love. Many people write books about topics that not only interest them but have special or personal meaning to them. After all, who would we be if we didn't have passion about our ideas?

That said, publishing is a business. And whether you plan to self-publish, use a hybrid publisher, or pursue a traditional publishing path, being able to sell your book is important. Not only do you want to make some money from your book, those who helped produce your book also have to get paid. Every book has a massive team behind it including editors, designers, production staff, marketing and PR specialists, and a host of others. Those people would not be employed if books did not sell in the marketplace. This isn't to say that capitalism is the only goal of selling a book. Sharing ideas, the freedom of speech, and helping people improve their lives with your words are all vital pursuits as well. But to do all that, you need to be able to sell your book, and that starts with determining if your book idea is viable. In this chapter, we'll talk about two ways to determine if your book idea can stand out in a flooded publishing market.

WHAT IS YOUR NICHE?

Can you pinpoint your book's niche? I assure you—there's really nothing new under the sun in the marketplace of ideas. The key is all in how you present that idea. So, think about your concept and your idea. Consider who else has written about it in both similar ways that are related to your outlook and conflicting ways that go against the grain of what your concept is. Now, where does your idea fit in here? In other words, what is your niche? Think about what your concept is and be able to affirm it in your pitch, the book itself, and how you eventually market it. Back in my grad school days, we were always encouraged to think of our essay topics as guests at a party. Everyone in the room is talking. Some people are saying things with which you agree. Some are dissenting voices to your worldview. Others are rehashing the same old conversations from the last party. Then you walk in. What can you say that is new and compelling? What is your unique contribution to the conversation? That's how you can think about your book's niche. Enter the room and say something different or new.

Let's go back to that hot air balloon idea for a minute. Say I want to write a very general book about hot air balloons, what they are, and how they work. That's too broad to be a book. But if I got very nichy and said, "Here's how I traveled the world in my hot air balloon," that's a very clearly defined subject. Plus, you've hit the right ethos note as well, since it's all about your own experience with the hot air balloon. You want to go narrow, not wide, which almost seems counterintuitive. One might think, "OK, if I want to sell a lot of books to a lot of people, I want my topic to be as broad as possible." But that's not always the case here. Remember: The riches are in the niches, so you want to get clear and very specific about your topic from the start.

WHAT IS YOUR USP?

In addition to a niche, your book idea also needs a unique selling proposition (USP). You might have heard this phrase used in the business world in regard to products and services. A USP is what makes your topic special and unique. Going back to the idea of a niche, how is your niche or your idea different than what's already out there? Maybe you're writing something that flies in the face of convention. Maybe you're writing something that no one has written about before. Maybe you're taking an old classic topic and putting a new spin on it for a new era or generation. You have to be able to define what it is that makes your niche and your approach special and different. As I mentioned earlier, have a narrow but deep focus. Take your niche and go deep to define what the unique benefit will be for your reader. Let's build onto the hot air balloon niche and add a layer. You can take the original niche (traveling in your hot air balloon) and add a benefit for your reader. Like this: "Here's how I traveled the world in my hot air balloon and how you can too." The "how you can too" is the USP of your book. Pretty nichy, right?

What makes it unique, perhaps, is that you can write about how much money is required to do this, what that lifestyle looks like, how to be in community with other people who are also traveling in the world in hot air balloons, etc. In other words, go very deeply into your topic's USP so that your potential agent, editor, or reader comes away thinking they simply must read this book.

IS IT A BOOK?

There are so many wonderful ideas out there, but not all of them are big enough to take up 200-300 pages of content that people will buy. You really have to be able to dive deeply into your niche, but you also have to have enough to say about it to warrant a full book-length work. Remember, not every idea is a book. Some ideas make great articles, blogs, or social posts, but there's just not enough "there" there for them to be a book. So, what should a book-length idea look like? Have that clearly defined subject in place. Your topic should not be so broad that it's hard to rein in, but not so small that you can't justify at least 35,000-40,000 words.

To determine if your book can make the stretch, let's revisit college comp class. Remember writing essays (or maybe you've blocked out the memory for sanity's sake)? In addition to a thesis statement, you had to have claims and evidence to support those claims and, thus, the thesis.

Think of your book idea in a similar way. Take your primary idea and see if you can make three to five major claims about it. In other words, what are the three to five big things you want to cover about your niche topic?

Next, think about possible evidence that can support your claims. No matter what your nonfiction book is about, quantifiable research is the proof in the pudding for your ideas. That doesn't mean that you have to be an academic by trade. It simply means that you need to be able to talk and write about your topic using solid information to back up what you say. So, in my hot air balloon book, I can't just say living the hot air balloon life is the best life ever because I said so. That's not enough. You need to be able to say, "Here are some really great ways that you can make a living while enjoying the hot air balloon life," or, "Here are some great ways that you can live this life without disrupting your finances, and I'm going to prove it to you because I've interviewed people and I have citations and I have sources." So quantifiable research really is about asking yourself whether you can back up what you say. Not every topic has to be written in a very academic way but at the very least you should be able to say:

- Here's some proof that my idea is legit.
- This is why my idea is doable.
- Here are the steps to make my idea work.
- This topic matters to a specific audience in a way that they can quantify.

Being able to say and expound on one or more of these helps you show that your book is, in fact, a unique offering for readers.

Quiz: Is It a Book?

Let's take a quick quiz to determine if your idea could be a book:

1. Is your idea based on your personal feelings about a topic or a singular experience?
2. Is your idea about a finite topic that requires some documentation or research that can reach a resolution in under 10,000 words?

3. Is your idea a new spin on an existing topic, a personal narrative about major events, or one that requires multiple claims and evidence points? Is it all three?

Starting with the first question, ask yourself if your idea really just your personal ruminations on a topic in which you have no quantifiable expertise. If so, then it's not a commercially viable book project. Consider question 2. Is your idea about a finite topic that requires a little bit of documentation that can reach a final conclusion or thesis in under 10,000 words? That my friend is an article. Finally, is your idea a new spin on a topic that already exists or perhaps a personal narrative about a series of events that lots of people know about, or maybe one that requires multiple claims and evidence points? In other words, is it going to take a lot of words to come to a resolution? Then you most likely have a book idea on your hands.

Want to learn more? Check out Episode 2 of the **Pub Date Podcast:** "Can I Develop My Idea Into A Book?" • To listen, visit: **bit.ly/PubDateEp2**

Activity 2
BOOK IDEA BRAINSTORM

Now that you have thought a little bit more about your idea, what it's niche and USP are, and whether or not it can be a book, it's time to do your second activity, the book idea brainstorm.

1. What is my concept?

....

....

....

2. Who am I?

....

....

....

3. What is my topic's USP?

....

....

....

4. What makes this idea exciting?

....

....

....

5. What are the 3-5 major points I can make about this idea?

....

....

....

....

....

....

STEP 3

Lay the Professional Groundwork

ONE OF THE MOST REWARDING PARTS of working with nonfiction book authors is seeing how their book fits into their broader content ecosystem. I love getting to know authors who are really digging into who they are and what they can become when they add a book to their already wide variety of expert offerings. Every nonfiction author is different, and everyone will have a different professional background as well as various activities and people they deal with as related to their book content. For example, a marketing expert who works with small business owners may have a thriving consulting business, do speaking engagements all over the country, appear at conferences, or even have a podcast. On the other hand, a crafter or maker who is highly active in the crafting community and who is interested in doing a book may teach classes at the local community college or perhaps offer online courses that teach people how to create beautiful quilts, make handmade soaps, or even bake the most delicious sourdough bread.

That's the beauty of the nonfiction book space. There are subject matter experts everywhere and in every topic area. With such a breadth and depth of knowledgeable experts all across the nonfiction category, it's no wonder that laying professional groundwork before you go out and pitch your book is an important step along your publishing journey. Don't get me wrong, that doesn't mean that you have to go out and be someone you are not. Quite the contrary! Laying professional groundwork before you pitch your book is really all about leaning into what you already know and do well. That's what we're going to cover in this chapter—leaning into the subject matter expert you already are.

THE THREE LAYERS OF PROFESSIONAL OUTREACH

Many authors I work with are often surprised to find that marketing for their book actually begins well in advance of finding a publishing path. It's certainly natural to assume that marketing doesn't happen until the book is produced and published, but that's not the case. Everything that you do as a subject matter expert leading up to the publishing of your book is important and a part of your overall book marketing process. Whether you are ready to pursue a book project right now or if it's part of a longer-term plan for your professional life, it's a good idea to go ahead and think about how you can create what I call a content ecosystem around your book. A *content ecosystem* is exactly what it sounds like, an ecosystem made up of all kinds of content that you can produce about your topic area. For example, if you work day-to-day in your subject matter area at a full-time job, you're already marketing yourself as a subject matter expert to colleagues whom you work with. If, for example, you are an entrepreneur then you are marketing yourself each and every day as a subject matter expert. Adding a book to the mix is a very natural progression for building on that content ecosystem.

The most successful subject matter expert authors start marketing themselves within that existing ecosystem, no matter how big or small it is. I always like to tell authors to market what you know, to people you know, where you are known. Remember these three layers of professional groundwork, and you'll be in good shape to eventually market your book:

- **What you know.** Practice being the subject matter expert in more places than just your everyday work life. Marketing what you know helps build your author and expert ethos. The more you talk about your expertise, how you apply it, and its value, the better position you will be to be accepted as an expert when you're writing a book. This isn't to say that you shouldn't also touch on topic areas that are adjacent to yours or that simply interest you—it's fine to do that but in terms of laying the professional groundwork for your book, really digging deeply into your subject matter area of expertise is an important skill to have.

- **To people you know.** Exploring your topic area with people you know is also a vital piece of this exercise. By "people you know," I don't mean that you are simply talking to friends, colleagues, and relatives, about your subject matter. By "people you know," I mean your intended audience for your book project. Who is interested in your topic area? Who follows you on social media or reads your articles or blogs? When you are promoting yourself professionally, you naturally want to promote yourself to people who are interested in what you have to say.

- **Where you are known.** As you expand your areas of influence as a subject-matter expert, you can niche down that wide net by focusing on areas in which you are known. By this, I mean talk to the people who want to hear what you have to say in places where it makes sense for you to say it. For example, if you are a subject matter expert in a scientific field, places you are known and followed would be journals, at professional events, at academic conferences, and even on social media geared toward people who follow influencers in your topic area. Or let's say that you are a chef known for creating wonderful dishes from foraged plants. That's a specific niche, but it has a dedicated audience. Perhaps you meet them where they are on social media, at enthusiasts' conventions, or even with a dedicated e-mail newsletter list. Choose mediums and content systems that make sense for not only who you are as a person and a professional but that also makes sense for your subject matter area.

I like to think of these three layers as guiding principles, not necessarily prescriptive steps that you take to build your professional content ecosystem. With every step you take to build up your professional ethos, that will be so important to you as you pitch to agents, editors, and potential business partners. Simply keep those three layers in mind to make sure that you're hitting all of those notes.

> Want to learn more? Check out Episode 25 of the **Pub Date Podcast:** "Get Your Author Platform Publication Ready with Emily Carpenter-Pulskamp" • To listen, visit: **bit.ly/ PubDateEp25**

CREATE AUTHENTIC CONNECTIONS

Once you have those three layers in mind, you can dig more into specific ways of connecting with your potential readers and market before you even approach a publisher. Let's get a bit more granular and cover more specific, authentic ways to lay your professional groundwork.

Connect (or Reconnect) with Your Target Network

Laying your professional groundwork starts with people first. Before you go out and start booking speaking engagements, setting up a social media profile, or thinking about who specifically you're going to sell your book to, first make sure that your name is on the lips of everyone in your immediate and adjacent networks. This doesn't mean that you should start marketing your book to these people directly at this point. Rather, engage with them in genuine and meaningful ways through the work you do, share the work you do, and build up others within your subject matter area of expertise. A holistic, genuine approach to connecting with people professionally matters here. Keep in mind that your connections and relationships should never be transactional, but rather value-added experiences for both parties involved. These are the groups of people who should be on your professional radar always, not just when you're promoting a book:

- **Colleagues.** Colleagues aren't just people you work with; they are people who are in your life for a reason just as you are in theirs for a reason. It's really easy to equate work colleagues with people whom we just see in the office or on Zoom every day, but I would encourage you to dive deeper into those relationships and focus on your shared joys and passions around your subject matter. Those with whom you work either directly or indirectly can be some of your biggest supporters and most valuable cheerleaders.

- **Clients.** Make a point to connect regularly with your clients, especially if you are a small business owner or entrepreneur. Your clients are the lifeblood of your business, and they should be treated with respect and kindness at all times. That doesn't mean that they are always right, but what it does mean is that they are valuable to you just as you are valuable to them. So, honor those relationships and connect often, even if it's not business focused. Send a holiday card, touch base every now and then just to see how they are doing, ask about their family. Building relationships outside of the transactional arena of business is important, especially with people with whom you are going to be working repeatedly. Remember that your clients are the recipients of your subject-matter expertise and knowledge, so there's no one better to support you when it comes time to write and promote your book.

- **Contemporaries.** Build strong relationships with others who are in your field or related areas of interest and expertise. One of the most gratifying parts of being a subject matter expert is getting to know other people in your field who are doing amazing work and sharing it. Meet people at conferences, follow your contemporaries on social media, read their books, and be as supportive of them as you would hope they would one day be supportive of you. I like to think of contemporaries as colleagues outside of the normal confines of work. These are people like you who have similar interests that sometimes overlap with yours. Have an abundance mindset when you are thinking about your contemporaries. They are not competitive with you, not really. Rather, they are fellow travelers on a similar professional journey.

- **Followers.** If you are lucky enough to already have a following of people who will be your ideal reader candidates in the future, that's great. Those who follow you either formally or informally are the people you want in your corner when it's time to promote your book. Perhaps you have a social media presence. Or maybe you write for journals or magazines and have the built-in readership already. Your followers can even be friends and family. All of these people already root for you and will be vital to the success of your book going forward. Connect with them often, connect with them about things that aren't necessarily related to your book project, and, like working with colleagues, create a holistic and rewarding relationship that is not transactional.

- **Influencers.** Do you work in a space that involves influencers? I bet you do. It's time to let go of the standard notion of an influencer is purely a social media figurehead. There are influencers everywhere, and they already have something that you are eventually going to need—street cred with a built-in audience. Become a student of the influencers in your field, whether on social media, print, or in other forms of media. Watch how they talk about your topic. Are there things that you like about how they present themselves? Are there things you don't? Tap into their world by becoming a follower yourself, so you can not only study how they promote themselves but so that you can engage with them as well.

Want to learn more? Check out Episode 28 of the **Pub Date Podcast:** "Build an Influencer Marketing Campaign with Lilian Sue" • To listen, visit: **bit.ly/PubDateEp28**

Amp Up Your Professional Visibility

Once you've reestablished your footprint with your existing network and potential target audience, focus on amping up your professional visibility as well. You can do this in all kinds of ways, from connecting more on LinkedIn to taking part in more visible means of connection through associations, speaking engagements, or other events. Here are a few great ways to increase your professional visibility not only to support a future book project, but to build your brand as a subject-matter expert:

- **Enhance your LinkedIn profile.** So many subject matter experts believe that LinkedIn is not a viable source of connection for them, but that couldn't be further from the truth. No matter what area you work in, there will be like-minded people for you to connect with on LinkedIn. But before we dive further into increasing your social media footprint, let's just start with the basics here. Make sure that your LinkedIn profile is well optimized not only for searchability but also for content. One of the best ways to do this is to focus on using keywords that resonate with your audience. Shine a light on your specific set of skills, especially as they relate to your book topic. For example, if your area of expertise is book publishing, like mine, I would want to focus on keywords that explore all of the different aspects of publishing in which I have expertise. You might use words like *editorial*, *profit and loss statement*, *forecasting*, *developmental editing*, or even *book production* and *design*. Those are words that are commonly used in our profession, so I know people will be searching for them and thus I want to use them somehow in my profile. That doesn't mean that you should not be honest about who you are and what you do, but if you know the buzzwords that are common in your industry, and you can weave them into your profile somehow, then do so.

Want to learn more? Check out Episode 11 of the **Pub Date Podcast:** "How to Promote Your Book on LinkedIn (without being salesy)" • To listen, visit: **bit.ly/PubDateEp11**

- **Write in your area of expertise.** Yes, you are already working on a book project, which is great! But in thinking about highlighting your writing skills, one great way to do that is to build up a portfolio of articles, essays, or scholarship. Are there magazines or publications in your area of expertise that you could pitch articles to? Maybe there are online sites that focus on a particular aspect of your content area where you could write an article. I would even argue that writing on sites like Medium or Substack and establishing a blog centered around your topic area is just as effective as getting bylines from other organizations. You don't have to be prolific as Shakespeare, but you should have some visibility in the writing world as it relates to your area of interest.

- **Speak at events.** Getting comfortable with being in front of people and talking about what you know is a vital skill for any potential book author. There are so many opportunities these days to go out and meet people and talk about your expertise. Even post pandemic, we are seeing a significant ramp-up of in-person events as well as online forums like webinars and online courses. Even hosting a seminar at your local library is a wonderful way to get started in the speaking world.

- **Collaborations.** Working together with colleagues and other notables in your field is a wonderful way to build your professional ethos. This doesn't mean that you have to do big, sweeping projects with people, but rather, take part in the community of knowledge that surrounds your topic area. It's really important to keep in mind that subject-matter experts don't live in a vacuum, nor do they do their work in one. No matter what your topic is, you are part of the community of thinkers, writers, and professionals in your field. So, take the time to connect with those people, talk with them, and find ways to work together. Or, if that kind of collaboration isn't in the cards for you, at the very least be an active participant in their professional world. I think you'll find a little goodwill goes a long way with colleagues, and eventually, you will have a host of people willing to support you professionally as well.

ENHANCE YOUR BRAND VISIBILITY

Next, let's talk about building up the visibility of your professional brand. Now before you throw up your hands and say, "A brand? I'm not a brand, I'm a person!" I want you to keep in mind that for the purposes of writing a book, yes—you are a brand. I'm not saying that to minimize your humanity—we're all human—but if you want to make your book a vital part of your content ecosystem, you need to look at that ecosystem with a business mindset. Your business (and, by extension, your book) IS your brand. Here are a few ways you can easily enhance your brand visibility, even if the word "brand" scares you.

Build a Professional Landing Page

Building a landing page for your professional life can help you highlight your work, engage with your audience, and ultimately grow your brand. You can keep the page fairly simple with an About Me page, links to your work and projects, social buttons, and a link to information about your book and offerings. If you want to get a little more in the landing page weeds, follow these steps:

- **Define your goals.** Determine what you want to achieve with it. Is it to promote your latest book, collect e-mail sign-ups for your newsletter, or simply to provide information about yourself and your work?
- **Decide where you want to host your landing page.** There are several options available, including website builders like WordPress, Wix, or Squarespace. Choose the platform that best fits your needs in terms of customization, ease of use, and cost.
- **Choose a theme.** Most website builders offer pre-designed templates or themes that you can customize to match your brand. Choose a template that aligns with the tone and style of your writing.
- **Write strong copy.** Your landing page copy should be clear, concise, and persuasive. Write a headline that grabs attention and clearly communicates the value proposition of your brand. Use persuasive language to highlight the benefits of your work and encourage visitors to act, whether it's buying your book, signing up for your newsletter, or following you on social media.
- **Use high-quality images that reflect your brand.** This could include author photos, book covers, or images related to the topics you write about. Avoid using generic stock photos and opt for authentic visuals that display your personality and style.

- **Include social proof.** Testimonials, reviews, and endorsements can help build credibility and trust with your audience. Include snippets of positive reviews from readers, endorsements from influencers or industry experts, or media mentions of your work.
- **Add a call to action (CTA).** Clearly define the action you want visitors to take on your landing page, whether it's to buy your book, sign up for your newsletter, or follow you on social media. Place a prominent CTA button above the fold and make it visually distinct so it stands out.
- **Collect data.** If your goal is to capture leads, integrate a form or opt-in box on your landing page where visitors can enter their e-mail address to subscribe to your newsletter or receive updates about your work. Keep the form fields minimal to reduce friction and increase conversions. This list will come in handy when it's time to market your book.

This structured approach to setting up a landing page will allow you to add more elements to it when it's time to promote your book.

> Want to learn more? Check out Episode 15 of the **Pub Date Podcast:** "Best Practices for Building Your Author Brand with Stephen A. Hart" • To listen, visit: **bit.ly/PubDateEp15**

Increase Your Social Footprint

You can increase your social media footprint by leveraging your expertise and sharing useful and informative content with your followers. the informational value of their content. Here are a few ways to do that:

- **Identify and understand your audience.** You can use your ideal reader as a guide when thinking about your audience. Keep them in mind here and focus on platforms where your audience is most active (LinkedIn for professionals, Facebook for broader audiences, etc.).

- **Create high-quality, informative content.** Share insightful articles, research findings, and industry news relevant to your book's topic. Focus on what your ideal reader might find interesting, like informative videos, infographics, and tutorials that provide value and demonstrate your expertise. Offer useful tips, advice, and practical applications related to your book's content.
- **Leverage different platforms for different audiences.** For example, you can use LinkedIn to publish thought leadership articles and engage in professional discussions. Is video your thing? Consider creating a YouTube channel or Instagram profile to share educational videos and visual content.
- **Engage with your audience.** Always be a good social steward of your brand by responding promptly and professionally to comments and messages. Ask questions and create polls to encourage discussions around your book's topics or host webinars, live Q&A sessions, and virtual workshops to interact directly with your audience.
- **Shift your networking focus to social media.** Partner with other experts, thought leaders, and influencers in your field for joint content and cross-promotion. Remember to give your followers useful and fun content like social media takeovers with other nonfiction authors or other industry experts. Take part in events such as LinkedIn discussions, Instagram takeovers, and Facebook group conversations.
- **Use industry-specific and trending hashtags to increase visibility and reach a broader audience.** You can create your own branded hashtag for your book concept to encourage followers to share their experiences with your content.
- **Promote exclusive content.** As you start to build your social brand, share exclusive content such as unpublished chapters, research data, or case studies to entice followers. Host giveaways or contests related to your book's theme to boost engagement and attract new followers so they are already engaged by the time you publish your book.

- **Run paid advertising campaigns.** You can run targeted ads on platforms like LinkedIn and Facebook to reach professionals and enthusiasts interested in your book's subject. Promote high-performing posts to increase their reach and attract more followers. Not sure about your social media advertising skills? Hire social media help on sites like Upwork to take the load off your plate.

These are just a few ways you can use social media to your professional advantage. Keep in mind that even if you are not yet in publishing mode, you can lay the professional groundwork to set yourself up for success, effectively building a larger and more engaged audience over time.

Activity 3
DESCRIBE YOUR PLATFORM

This is your opportunity to show the agent or editor that you have marketing plans in place. Ideally, this section is combined with the author bio information and is 2-4 pages long.

1. Online presence

....

....

....

....

....

....

....

....

....

....

....

....

....

2. Content production

....

....

....

....

....

....

....

....

....

....

....

....

....

3. E-mail lists

....
....
....
....
....
....
....
....

4. Social media

....
....
....
....
....
....
....
....
....

5. Events and speaking

....
....
....
....
....
....
....
....
....

6. Media appearances

7. Memberships and associations

8. Connections and endorsements

STEP 4

Conduct Research

IT MAY BE HARD TO BELIEVE, but research is a really important part of how you write a book proposal. And you thought you were done doing research when you left high school or graduated college! Wrong! You don't have to be a book publishing professional to conduct strong research to help you write your book proposal. You just need to know how to qualify and quantify a little bit about your audience and your competition. In addition, you need to have a good idea of what kind of publishers might be interested in your book. Or, if you're planning to self-publish, or go the hybrid route, you should know what type of publishing partners are a good fit for your particular topic. In this chapter, we'll talk a little bit about how to do that research. From identifying your reader avatar to creating a target list of publishers or publishing partners, you'll be ready to craft a plan for your publishing path that fits you best and best serves the needs of your project.

DEVELOP A READER AVATAR

What is a reader avatar? It is not a character from a popular James Cameron movie—at least not in this case. Your reader avatar is a representation of your ideal reader. In fact, you can have more than one reader avatar for your book project. I like to have 3 to 4 in place so that I have a good firm understanding of the breadth and depth of my potential audience for a book. Let's talk about each one in detail.

Primary Reader

Your primary reader is going to be the avatar that is most inclusive of who your ideal reader may be. In other words, they are the customer whom you describe as the perfect reader for your book. They hit all the notes for you as a potential customer. They are:

- Already engaged with your content area of expertise
- A follower of your work or your colleague's work
- Someone who already buys books in your category
- An enthusiast of your content area
- Someone who will likely buy more books by you in the future
- A reader who may need your content to further their own professional development

Your primary reader is the person to keep in mind as you are crafting your book project because they are likely to be your most ardent supporter and longtime reader or potential client.

Secondary Reader

Your secondary reader is what I would consider a tertiary reader. By this, I mean that they have a related interest in your book, your topic area, or you as a subject-matter expert, but they may not know you well enough yet to be a dedicated, longtime fan. A secondary reader might buy your book for a variety of reasons, including:

- They need it for a class or for work.
- They heard about you or read about you in the media and are curious about your topic.
- They read competitive works in your content area and are curious about your take on a subject. They have a dedicated

interest in your content area or topic and tend to purchase any books about it.

The great thing about secondary readers is if you hook them with great content and a compelling book, they have the potential to become long-term readers or even potential clients. I don't know about you, but I have purchased many a book that I was simply curious about only to turn into a follower of that particular writer, anxiously awaiting their next book project.

Topic-Curious Reader

A topic-curious reader is someone who may be new to you and your content area. Perhaps they have heard about the topic you write about and are starting to explore it more. Or maybe they are a novice enthusiast or scholar just getting to know your content area. Here are some examples of a topic-curious reader:

- Someone picking up a new hobby
- A person who heard about your topic via a media source and wants to dig in deeper
- A reader who is already engaged with similar topics and is branching out

I love topic-curious readers! Aren't we all topic-curious about most things anyway? There is truly little under the sun that each of us knows enough about to consider ourselves an expert. Your topic-curious readers often have outsized enthusiasm about self-education and learning, which makes them highly active readers.

Whim Reader

Who among us hasn't grabbed a book from an endcap or point-of-purchase display because the cover or title grabbed our attention? This is what your whim reader will do. A whim reader didn't come to the bookstore looking for your book—they happened upon it. A whim reader may be:

- Picking up something in the airport bookstore to get them through a long flight
- Grabbing a book with a cover that compelled them to purchase
- Intrigued by a well-versed title
- Choosing a book for a special occasion gift

A whim reader is the "choose your own adventure" reader—you never know where your book may take them. They may become dedicated fans, or they may find that your content isn't for them.

Keep all of these potential reader avatars in mind as you craft your book concept and later, your proposal. Remember: You don't have to be all things to all readers. That said, having a picture in your mind of who your potential readers may be can help you contextualize your pitch and your proposal.

STUDY YOUR COMPETITION

Before you dig into writing your proposal, which we'll do in the coming chapters, I want you to take some time to study your competition on the bookshelves. One of the most important sections you will write in your book proposal is about competitive titles and how your title is different from those. Taking some time to research similar titles sets you up for success when it's time to write that section of your proposal. Plus, it gives you good insight into how best to position your book whenever you talk about it with potential publishers, agents, or publishing partners.

Speak from a place of education and knowledge about how your book fits into a broader conversation around your topic area. Whether you're writing a profoundly serious book that perhaps is academic in nature, or you're writing a cookbook, or even a book about crafting or cooking, you should know where your voice fits into the broader conversation among your publishing peers. When you interact with potential stakeholders like agents, publishers, or publishing partners, a big part of what you will express to them is how your book is unique, different, and an important addition to the current content landscape. Knowing more about other people who write in your content area helps you do that because it allows you to position yourself as a unique voice with something new to say.

When you research the competition in preparation for positioning your own work, focus on a few key competitive works. How do you know if a book is a competitive title? You can start figuring that out by looking at books with similar themes and topics. What other books are out there that are adjacent to your topic area or about the same topic but maybe with a slightly different twist than yours?

You can also look at authors whom you admire in your topic space or whom you want to emulate. These are naturally competitive titles. Also consider exploring authors with whom you disagree. Look, too, for adjacent themes. These are topics that are similar to yours or in a closely related content area. For example, if I'm writing a book about a psychological topic, I may want to pull some books about the sociological ramifications of that topic and use those as competitive themes and competitive books.

Competitive titles don't have to be books that are exactly like yours. Competitive titles can be related to your topic area, or about a similar topic in the same space but with a different point of view. They can even be books that come at a shared topic from a vastly different, divergent angle. That said, they should be similar in approach or scope (that's the relational piece). For example, if you're writing a book that's intended for the consumer market for the everyday reader, you wouldn't necessarily want to compare it to a textbook. Those are a different category of books altogether, so try to keep like with like. Think "related, but different." One way I like to do this is to not only look at what the book descriptions are on online book retailer sites, but also look for books that are similar in price range and in page count.

You can compare your book to those from big-ticket authors who you know have a ton of sales, but I would also go a little bit deeper and go beyond the people you see at the top of that bestseller list every day. Include some mid-list or independent authors as well in your research who compete with you in your category. Your list of competitive authors doesn't have to just be Malcolm Gladwell-type books or the latest offering from today's hottest celebrity chef. There should be a little bit of everything in the mix.

Competitive titles can (and should) also be by divergent authors who view the world and your topic differently than you do. These are important to include if they are available because it really shows that you know what the greater landscape of that topic looks like. Having a good grasp of what else is on the shared bookshelf will help you best position your own work, how you pitch it, and how you find the best publishing pathway for it.

RESEARCH PUBLISHING OPTIONS

The final piece of initial research I encourage you to do before you jump into writing your proposal is researching your publishing options. I've already mentioned throughout the book that you have options. Everyone's publishing path is unique to them, and yours is no different. Depending on your publishing goals, you may choose to go the traditional route and seek an agent that will pitch you to a publisher. Perhaps you want to go a little bit smaller and work with an independent publishing house or a hybrid publisher, where you put some money in to the project and so do they. Or, perhaps you want to control the entire process as well as retain your intellectual property. Then self-publishing is the route for you. Let's dig a little more into how you can start to research each of your options.

Self-Publishing

Let's start with the choice which gives you the most creative control. Self-publishing has come a long way over the years. In the heyday of traditional publishing, self-publishing was almost a dirty word. There were a lot of vanity presses out there taking advantage of authors, doing nothing more than typesetting their book and slapping a cheap cover on it. While those bad actors remain in the game, there are now several viable options for self-publishing that provide you with a quality product and a quality experience.

These days, authors who self-publish are really stepping into the driver's seat of the publisher role. In other words, your book truly is your business, and you need to think like a publisher. That means that you are not only interested in producing a quality book, but you're also interested in marketing it yourself, being the public face of your own publishing brand, and doing all the legwork that a publisher would do. Self-publishing is no longer about selling books out of the back of your trunk. Self-publishing now is about you, the author, being the head of your business brand.

My advice to authors who want to get involved in self-publishing is to do just that, be the boss of your book. Start by exploring vendors and publishing partners who have a long history of producing quality book products. That said, not every author has a publishing background and knows exactly how to produce a quality book on their own. That's where vendors and packagers come into play. There are several quality book packagers out there today who work exclusively with self-published authors to produce a great product that they can feel proud of. When you're researching potential self-publishing partners or packagers, here are some questions to ask:

- What kind of publishing experience does the vendor have? Their website should highlight not only their publishing history but also include a portfolio of successful projects on which they have worked.
- Who are their other clients? Do they publish books in your area or in areas related to it?
- What do they offer as a part of their package? Will they edit your book? Do they design the interiors and the cover? Will they take care of setting up your ebook for distribution? What about getting an ISBN or a barcode? Make sure you know what is included as a part of the deal.
- Do they have any testimonials or recommendations from happy clients?
- Are they a part of any professional associations like the Independent Book Publishers Association (IBPA) or the American Book Producers Association (ABPA)?
- What is their pricing structure, and is it in your budget?

These are all things to keep in mind as you explore whether self-publishing is for you. You may find as you conduct your research that self-publishing isn't quite what you're looking for. Maybe you need someone to add marketing support or public relations support for your book. Most packagers do not offer that as a service, so you would have to explore that piece of the publishing journey with a different vendor. Or perhaps self-publishing is exactly what you want because you want to be your own publisher, have your own imprint, or simply control the creative side as well as the business side of your book.

Hybrid Publishing

Hybrid publishing is exactly what it sounds like—it's the best of both worlds. In hybrid publishing, authors help fund the book while the publishing partner also puts in money toward the project. The difference between hybrid publishing and traditional publishing is this, along with the fact that as an investor in the project you will likely get a higher royalty structure. Putting some skin in the game not only shows your commitment to the project but also makes you a vital business partner in the publishing venture.

Like self-publishing, hybrid publishing has come a long way in the last few years. Many publishers are realizing that running a traditional advance and royalty structure while facing increased discount requirements from retailers is a fiscally challenging prospect. Because of this, many publishers are offering hybrid models now in which the author helps fund the initial project. This could mean that the author pays for the actual printing of the book, or it could mean that they pay for an outside editor or a freelance design artist. In this scenario, the author typically receives higher royalties on the back end. Whereas in traditional publishing when you don't put skin in the game, your royalty structure is much smaller down the line.

When exploring potential hybrid publishers and trying to determine if that's the right path for you, start by exploring some of those publishers' websites to see how they position themselves as hybrid publishers. What do they offer? What kind of support will there be for you as an author when it comes to marketing and selling the book? What does their distribution model look like? Do they pursue subsidiary or ancillary rights on your behalf, like foreign rights or audio rights? Where does your financial commitment end and theirs begin? And how does that look once revenue starts coming in from retailers? What kind of reception do their books get in the publishing world? Are they well regarded and well reviewed? What is their track record and what is their street cred?

I think you'll find that you don't have to be a millionaire to pursue hybrid publishing. Most hybrid publishing deals are quite fair and provide you with the best of both worlds by having some creative control and getting the marketing support that would be more common with a traditional publisher.

Traditional Publishing

Traditional publishing is a vast, vast landscape. When you start to research potential publishers and agents in the traditional publishing space, there is a lot of information to wade through. Before digging more deeply into that research, consider revisiting what your goals are for your publishing journey. What do you really want out of this process? Is it simply to have a book with your name on it? Do you have hopes of being widely distributed or perhaps getting your book translated into other languages? Revisit on those goals and see if they truly align with what a traditional publishing experience looks like. Keep in mind, traditional publishing is a highly competitive landscape and getting more so every day. This is especially true for nonfiction books. So, if this is the game that you want to be in, you'd better be ready to play.

There are a lot of great resources out there that you can use to begin to research publishers and agents. Start by researching publishers and agents who work in your content area. It's important to keep in mind that not every publisher publishes every topic under the sun. Nor do agents represent everything under the sun. Some houses and agents specialize only in fiction, which is a completely different ball game than what we're talking about here. Some publishers have a niche approach and only publish in a few certain topic areas and not broad nonfiction. The same is true for agents. The riches are in the niches, remember, so not every agent will represent a wide variety of content areas. Here are some places you can start your research journey when it comes to traditional publishing:

- Publishing guide books like *Jeff Herman's Guide to Book Publishers, Editors, & Literary Agents* (New World Library)

- Trade magazines and websites like *Publishers Weekly* or *Publishers Lunch*
- Association of American Publishers (AAP)
- Independent Book Publishers Association (IBPA)
- PubWest
- Book Industry Study Group (BISG)
- Association of American Literary Agents (AALA)
- Association of Authors' Representatives (AAR)
- Acknowledgment pages of competitive titles

Regardless of what kind of publishing path you choose to research, stay organized. I find that a simple Excel spreadsheet of all the tidbits I need to know about each of these potential pathways can be really useful. Or, if you just want to take notes in a notebook and go the Luddite path, that's completely fine, too. Whatever works for you is great, as long as you can compile your research and information in a way that makes sense to you so you can refer back to it later. It's going to come in really handy when it's time to write that proposal, which is what we'll do next.

Before moving on to the next chapter, take a moment to begin to scaffold your competitive analysis. As you'll read later, this is a vital part of your book proposal. Use the research that you've already done on competitive titles to get started by listing those titles and their pertinent information as well as a brief summary. In Step 7, we'll add more elements to the competitive analysis.

Activity 4
WRITE A COMPETITIVE ANALYSIS

Use this worksheet to draft each competitive title analysis. Your proposal should include at least 3-5 comp titles.

Title ....

Author ....

Publisher ....

Publication date .... **Price** ....

Page count and trim size ....

1. Book summary

....

....

....

....

....

....

2. Strengths and weaknesses of the competitive title

....

....

....

....

....

3. How is my book better/different?

....

....

....

....

....

....

Plan Your Proposal

I HAVE WORKED WITH nonfiction writers for over 25 years. From scientists and entrepreneurs to crafters and tech experts, the one question I have fielded more than any is, "Why do I need a book proposal?" As the publishing landscape has evolved over the years, so has my answer to that question.

In the era of "big" publishing in the 90s and early 2000s, many authors were chasing traditional deals with mid-to-large publishers. Small presses tended to stick more to specialty or regional fare, while university presses dug into the "publish or perish" engine of highly academic niche works. Self-publishing had a distinctly negative connotation, conjuring ideas of vanity presses that churned out low-quality, barely edited editions on bottom-of-the-barrel paper. Then, with the dawn of disruptive online retail models (you know the one I mean) and e-reader technology, we started to see a shift in how people thought about publishing. If the channels through which we bought books and the mediums by which we read them could be disrupted, so could how we created them. We started to witness a massive shift in the makeup of publishers and how they did business, resulting in a move toward a more democratized publishing model that is still evolving.

In those days of "big" publishing, where the big-or-bust mentality ruled, I would have told an author they had to have an agent before they could pitch to a house, and that their proposal was for the agent's, then editor's, eyes only. I would have said that having a proposal to pitch to an indie press was useful but not always necessary. And as for self-publishing? That was not for "serious" authors. But times change.

Today, my answer has shifted. Yes, if you are seeking an agent or a deal from a large house, the need and process remain largely unchanged. The audience is the same, for the most part. Indie presses now together comprise a larger market share than the "Big 4." And yes—you need a proposal to pitch to them. Hybrid publishers (which many presses both large and small are) want to know that you are a good author partner who will help market your book. They want to see your proposal. And, in that continued spirit of democratization, self-publishing is now a viable alternative for those authors who wish to retain creative control of their intellectual property (though you should still vet service providers carefully). You are the publisher in this case, and you will want a proposal to serve as a business plan for yourself and your book. No matter what path you choose, a book proposal is an important tool for you. In this chapter, we'll cover the finer points of what you can expect to see in your book proposal.

WHY YOU NEED A PROPOSAL

Let's talk a little bit more about why you need a book proposal. There are a lot of good reasons to have a proposal. For example, you might want to pitch your book to agents. Maybe you want someone to go out there and represent you to editors and publishing houses and negotiate on your behalf, or maybe you want to take your book directly to an independent publisher to see if they're interested in publishing it. Perhaps you are planning to self-publish or work with a custom publisher so you can retain creative control and your intellectual property rights, but you still want to map out a business plan for your book. All of these are great reasons to craft a solid book proposal. Think of this as a living document that you can use throughout the life of your book as a roadmap designed to help you navigate the lifecycle of your book project.

No matter your "why," it's important to remember that you also need a proposal to help you go out and sell the book with a strong story to tell. Your book proposal is just as much for you as it is for anybody else because it can help you do a few things:

- **Develop your elevator pitch and flesh out your proof of concept.** Let's say that your book idea is a bit nebulous at this point. A book proposal is going to help you dig into the content and think hard about what you want to say about your topic and how you're going to say it.
- **Engage with competitive and related titles.** Taking the step to dive deeply into the competitive publishing landscape for your book will help you get a better idea of what your niche is in the broader marketplace of ideas. One of the pieces in a book proposal we've already touched on is setting up a competitive analysis. In other words, go out and see what else is out there on the shelf. Who's written books that are similar to yours or maybe fly in the face of your idea? What books are on the other side of the fence from your idea? What books are written by people you admire who are writing in your same topic area?
- **Firm up your table of contents.** Maybe you know your main idea and you have three or four main points that you want to say about it. Now is your chance to hit the ground running and solidify specific chapters and how you will organize them.
- **Tell a story about why you are the right person to write this book.** What is your expertise? What is your platform (by platform, I mean how do you reach other people)? This is the place to share your book origin story.
- **Create a marketing plan that speaks to your strengths as a subject-matter expert in places where you engage fully with potential readers.** For example, maybe you don't do a whole lot on Facebook or Instagram, but you have a huge following on LinkedIn where you talk about your topic area or your ideas. A book proposal helps you highlight that and how you are going to use that particular social media niche to get out the word

about your book, gain followers, and get people to buy the book.

WORKING WITH DECISION MAKERS

Crafting a strong pitch and proposal is especially vital to your publishing journey when it comes to working with decision makers and stakeholders. This is true no matter what path you choose, from self-publishing to a fully traditional press experience. Going through the exercise of drafting a proposal forces you to think deeply about your project's scope and commercial potential with business partners, editors, and even yourself (yay, inner monologue!). Remember: Books aren't published in a vacuum so whether you want to self-publish, work with a hybrid publisher, or go traditional, you will need to engage with publishing professionals. A book proposal helps you prepare for any of these potential publishing pathways.

Once you send out a book proposal to potential partners or editors, you don't just get a "yes" or "no" via e-mail and off you go. Your potential business partner, editor, or agent will want to talk to you to learn more about the project, so a book proposal helps you have a good, firm proof of concept. Your proposal helps you talk in quantifiable terms about what this book is about so you can have those conversations going forward with even more stakeholders, like buyers and readers.

Let's talk a little bit more about who these stakeholders are and who the book proposal is for, besides you. A good proposal is for a lot of different people at many different stages of your editorial journey. First of all, the person who's probably the top of your mind is the primary decision maker like an agent, editor, or other publishing partner. Internal decision makers like the publisher's sales team, marketing team, and even the finance team will also have interest in your proposal.

Why the finance team? Well, this is a business after all, and the people in charge of the money are going to want to know if your book is going to make any. At a hybrid or traditional house, your editor works with the finance team to create something called a P&L, or a profit and loss statement. This document estimates how the book is going to perform in the marketplace, how well it is going to sell, the price point, and costs associated with editorial and production. All of these numbers are flowing in the background while you're engaged in negotiations with the editor because at the end of the day, a publisher wants to make money. I assume you do as well.

Once you decide to get an agent, self-publish, or you are placed with a small independent house, hybrid partner, or a large publisher, there are other people who will want to see your book proposal. This includes foreign rights partners who shop your book for translation rights in other countries to overseas publishers. They'll want to take a look at the proposal so they, too, can get an idea of what that book is about so they can effectively sell rights on your behalf. Audio publishers could also be in the mix here. Keep in mind that not every publishing house produces their own audio books. Most publishing houses outsource that service to a third party, and for audio book publishers to say "yes" to a project, they need to have a firm idea of what the book is about. Finally, subsidiary rights partners might also want to take a look at your book proposal. These types of subsidiary rights partners can range from magazine editors to publishers who produce special anthologies or collections and have an interest in using a chapter or a portion of your book.

As you can see, no matter what kind of publishing path you take, you will encounter several types of decision makers along the way who could have interest in checking out your proposal. While your book is the cornerstone of your content ecosystem, it can lead to so many other lines of revenue for you as an author. The proposal is the front door that you will use to welcome in potential investors and partners who want to explore those areas of revenue potential.

THE PARTS OF A PROPOSAL

Now that you know the "why" behind a book proposal, let's dive into planning one by covering the specific parts of a nonfiction book proposal. Then, in the next two chapters, we will get more granular about what to include in each section.

A good proposal is made from a few working parts, but I like to categorize them into two main buckets: The "Are You a Good Writer?" part and the "Are You a Good Marketer?" part.

The "Are You a Good Writer?" Part

The "Are You a Good Writer?" part of your proposal highlights not only your ability to write well, but also your ability to organize and present your ideas well. Here are the sections of the proposal that address this part of your author ethos:

- **The overview.** This introductory section serves as a hook and a summary to draw the reader in. To clarify, I don't mean the end reader (the person who will buy your book off the shelf). I mean the agent, editor, or potential publishing partner whose attention you are hoping to grab by drawing them into your proposal and get them interested and excited about the commercial viability of your ideas.

- **Sample table of contents.** Keep in mind that your table of contents is a living, breathing thing. Once you decide to self-publish, go with an independent publisher, or if you get picked up by a bigger publisher, that table of contents will likely change as the book develops through the editorial process. But you want to make it as final as possible at this point, so your reader has a good feel for what you're covering in your book and what the topic areas pertain to your thesis/book concept.

- **Chapter summaries.** Provide descriptions for each chapter. These should be one to three paragraph descriptions that lay out what that chapter is about. I like to think of these as mini overviews for every single chapter, or a short elevator pitch.

- **Sample chapters.** You might wonder why it is that when authors or agents pitch fiction books, they are usually completely written, but nonfiction books aren't. One of the reasons is that nonfiction books often come into development as a concept to back up a brand (which is you, the author and subject-matter expert) or a concept that has strong marketability to its target audience. Editors and agents want to work with you to refine that idea and make it applicable to the specific marketplace you're trying to reach. An author will rarely turn in a fully realized, fully written nonfiction book at this point in the process. However, stakeholders and decision makers want to see if you can, in fact, write. So, a sample chapter or two is a vital element to include here.

The "Are You a Good Marketer?" Part

Next, your proposal will dig into your ability to help market your book. No matter what publishing path you choose, you will need to be an active participant in selling your book. Your job as an author does not end when you turn in your manuscript. Here are the sections of the proposal that help you show off your book marketing chops:

- **Market analysis.** This is where you are going to talk about the generalized market for your topic idea and how your book fits into it. The research rubber meets the road here because you are going to have to dig deeply into what your particular market looks like and back it up with some data points. For example, you might say the market for this book includes XYZ stakeholder groups or a particular reader avatar. Maybe you include some statistics that back up the need for your topic as a book. For example, if you're writing a book about podcasting, you might include some statistics about how many people have subscribed to or started podcasts in the last year to show that there is a hunger and a need for that particular topic area.
- **Competitive analysis.** Speaking of analysis, you're going to do some more in this section! Your competitive analysis is where you list some different books from your topic area that are similar to your book or somehow adjacent to your topic. This could include books that are in the same area or content space or those by authors whose approach is similar in scope to what you do. Don't just list these books. Go a little bit deeper by listing the details of the books like the publishing company, the year of publication, page count, and price. Then go deeper yet again to give a summary for each book and why your book is better or different.
- **Author platform.** This section is where you lay out your current market/audience reach. Note that I said "current" here. This is

not an aspirational section that spitballs what you want to do. This section is all about what you *already* do to market yourself as a subject-matter expert. For example, if you have a landing page that's attached to "expert" you or your business, you'll mention that and say how many people visit that website. Talk a little bit about your social reach, too, as well as speaking events and whether there are opportunities to buy books at those events. You'll also discuss your e-mail list. Do you have one? If so, how many people are on it? This section is where you give firm, quantifiable numbers to your readers so they can envision what the sales strategy might look like for your book with the resources you already have in place.

- **Marketing plan.** Here's where you outline how you are going to use that author platform to help promote and sell your book. Gone are the days when authors were given carte blanche to a PR team and were sent on book tours by their publishers. This is not the reality for the great majority of authors. Your book **is** your business, no matter what publishing path you take from self-publishing to traditional. Say what you're going to do to go out there and sell this book. Like the marketing platform, this also is not an aspirational section. This is where you say, "This is what I can do to promote by book with the resources and reach I have now." For example, if you don't have a website yet, don't put it in your marketing plan. Don't say, "I'm going to make a website and it's going to get X hits a day." You don't know that for sure. But what you can say is, "I'm going to develop a website and use these tools I already have in place to get more traffic to my emerging website." Have a specific plan with strong, quantifiable information. Bonus points if you can share a recent product launch strategy with results.

SCAFFOLD YOUR PROPOSAL

Now, before you have a panic attack about putting all of this information together (and it is **a lot** of information), take a few moments to remind yourself that you are an expert in your field. You **are** the right person to write this book. You just need to tell that story to yourself and anyone else who will be a stakeholder in your book project. So, before you stare at a blank page with a blinking cursor and talk yourself out of it, remember to eat the proposal elephant one bite at a time. You are not going to write it in one sitting.

To help yourself tackle writing the proposal, I recommend that you "scaffold" the project in two ways. First, plan it out in digestible chunks so that you can mark off a to-do list as you go. Then, once you've planned your time, you can "prewrite" each section using your planning method of choice, like outlining or mind mapping.

Plan Your Time

A typical book proposal ranges from 10-50 pages, based on the level of detail you provide and the length of your sample chapter. Most that come across my desk hit the 25-to-35-page mark, but your mileage may vary. Regardless, it's a big project, and you'll want to schedule out time to write it. Here are a few tips my authors have used over the years to help them plan their proposal writing time:

- **Create a time estimate for each section of your proposal.** Some sections take longer than others to write. For example, writing your sample chapter is going to take significantly longer than writing your author bio. Consider taking each section, then mapping out approximately how long you think will take to write it.
- **Provide yourself with a mini deadline for each section of the proposal.** Is your goal to write a proposal in a month? Or perhaps a week? Think about the total amount of time that you want to spend and then create a schedule from there.
- **Remember, you don't have to write the proposal in order.** It's OK to jump around as you are drafting it. In fact, I would advise strongly against writing it in the order that the sections naturally fall in the final proposal. Instead, think of each section of the proposal as its own mini project. That way, you can focus solely on the purpose and point of that individual section and give it your full attention before moving on to the next section.

- **Align your writing time with the time of day that you feel most productive.** For some people, that's in the morning before they get up to go to work or send the kids off to school. For others, afternoons may be the ideal time. Some folks even like to write at night when the house is quiet and everybody else has settled down for the evening. Lean into what works best for you and make that your prime writing time.
- **If you are having trouble concentrating as you write, try the time-chunking method.** Set aside mini blocks of time throughout your day to complete some of your writing tasks. Then allow yourself a small reward time period. For example, say you want to write your author bio in one day. Set aside small 20-to-30-minute blocks of time throughout the day to focus on nothing else. Do not check e-mail, do not make a phone call, and definitely do not scroll social media. Set your alarm, go hard for those 20 or 30 minutes, and then when time is up walk away and give yourself a break.

Prewrite Your Sections

Diving into a writing project like a book proposal can feel overwhelming, especially if you've never written one. How do you overcome the fear of getting started? You just start. One technique I recommend to potential authors is to prewrite each section of your proposal.

Let's go back to college for a minute. Do you remember outlining an essay? Or perhaps you used a mind map to organize your thoughts around a topic. Those skills from Composition 101 can be useful to you now so you can have a strong scaffold for each section before you start to expand your thoughts and words. Here are a few prewriting techniques that have worked for many of my authors over the years:

- **Good, old-fashioned outlining.** Build out a simple structure for your proposal with letter, number, and roman numeral headings signifying your primary points, evidence to back it up, and any anecdotal information you want to share. For example, when scaffolding your author platform section, you could make each primary outline heading a medium (social media,

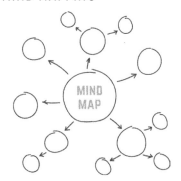

website, corporate connections, etc.), then each subsection your data points (social media followers, website traffic, speaking engagements and attendance), then add any colorful or useful anecdotes as your third tier of the outlined sections ("I speak at X Conference each year and have been asked back X number of years").

- **Mind mapping.** This is for those who love good visuals and think in images rather than lists. It's basically an outline, but in visual form. You can go old school and draw it (some folks think better when they have a tactile way to express themselves) or you can drop a flowchart into Word or PowerPoint. I like some of the online mind mapping software like MindMeister that allows you to make it a living document that can be changed as your project changes.
- **Voice memos.** Create a new voice memo for each section of your proposal. It can often help to talk yourself through what you want to write and can help that blank page and blinking cursor look less intimidating. Remember: This is for your ears only, so you can be as casual in your language as you like.
- **The Post-It wall.** Grab three different colors of Post-It Notes: One each for your primary points, evidence/data, and anecdotes. You can use these to create a visual outline on your office wall that will help you visualize what you want to include in each section. I love using this method because you can easily see your entire concept on one wall and move around bits and pieces as needed.

Now that you have a basic idea of what each section of the proposal is all about, it's time to create your own proposal prewrite. Using any of the methods above, go ahead and dive in. In the next two chapters, we'll dig more deeply into best practices for fleshing out the sections when it comes time to write the final product.

Activity 5
CREATE YOUR PROPOSAL PREWRITE

Use the following sections to map out a quick proposal prewrite. Feel free to use what works best for you: bullet points, lists, freewriting, mind mapping, etc. You'll use this as a basis for the full proposal later.

1. Book overview

2. Proposed table of contents

....
....
....
....
....
....
....
....
....
....
....
....
....
....
....

3. Chapter overviews and idea for your sample chapters

....
....
....
....
....
....
....
....
....
....
....
....
....
....
....
....
....
....

4. Market analysis

5. Competitive title analysis

6. Author platform

7. Proposed marketing plan

Write the Book Proposal, Part 1: Focus on the Book

A CONCERN MANY NONFICTION AUTHORS bring to me is that they don't feel they are "true" writers, and they are concerned that their fears about writing will keep them from finishing their book project. If that's how you feel, let me stop you right there. If you write, if you have a book idea that you can execute on; if you have done any prewriting to dream about what your book could be, then you **are** a writer. You don't have to be as gifted with language as Virginia Woolf or as prolific as James Patterson. You just have to write to be a writer.

That said, I understand the concern. Nonfiction writers are, by definition, voices of authority in their areas of expertise—not necessarily experts in writing and composition. As a subject-matter expert, you have a certain ethos by which you operate in the professional world. You ARE the expert in your field. That's a big deal, because it's how you will persuade your audiences—not only the one for your book, but the one (or ones) who will read your pitch and proposal. Your experience matters.

To best convey that experience, though, you need to be able to write about it in a way that is clear, concise, and descriptive enough all at the same time. No pressure, right? The "Are You a Good Writer?" part of the proposal is where you do that. In this chapter, we'll cover best practices for crafting a table of contents, outlining chapter summaries, writing a sample chapter, and composing a compelling overview. Let's get started!

THE TABLE OF CONTENTS

First on deck for the "Are you a good writer?" part of your proposal is the table of contents (TOC). This is where you map out what you feel is the best vision for your book. A strong TOC showcases to the reader that you have a firm grasp of your topic and how you're going to relay that structurally.

When you are thinking about creating a table of contents, first think about all of the working parts that you see in other nonfiction books and determine if they apply to your project. First of all, will there be a foreword in the book? A foreword is a useful marketing tool, especially if it's written by somebody who is a thought leader or who is known in the same topic area in which you write. A foreword is also useful if its author has really great name recognition in your field or with your audience. Make sure to assign the foreword to someone who meets those qualifications. You wouldn't want to assign a foreword to someone who's a casual acquaintance or a family member who is, of course, going to say nothing but laudatory things about you. A foreword should do some of that, but mostly explore the topic and why you are the best person to write about it.

A foreword does a couple of things for your book. First, it ties you to somebody notable who can go out and help market the book. It can also work as a lengthier testimonial that says to readers, "Hey, this person thought this book was great, so maybe I will give it a try." If you have someone to write a foreword who meets those criteria, go ahead and put them in the table of contents but only if it's confirmed. For example, if there's a thought leader whom you admire greatly and you're going to approach them about writing the foreword but they have not said yes yet, don't list them in your table of contents. Only add forewords by people who are confirmed.

Next in the TOC, let's include an introduction. This is one I also get a lot of questions about. Authors don't always understand the purpose of or need for an introduction, often assuming it is "fluff" that doesn't serve a purpose. I think the introduction is actually a wonderful tool for your reader that can help them step into your topic, get to know who you are, and set expectations for what is to come in the book. The introduction to your book doesn't operate as a first chapter. Rather, it operates as the groundwork you're going to lay for your overall topic. It introduces people to the book and the overall concept by perhaps positing a question about why this book is important and why it matters. Maybe it tells a little bit of the background or origin story of your idea. It doesn't give away the whole story, but it hints at it.

Then, your TOC should dive right into the chapters of your nonfiction book. For most nonfiction books, Chapter One tends to be an overview or broader introduction into the book itself. It is similar to a survey course chapter, digging deeply into your thesis statement or your main idea and making the case for the purpose of the book. Chapter One also does some groundwork and further fleshes out what big topics are to come in future chapters as they relate to the broader notes and takeaways of the books' thesis. This isn't to say that the first chapter of a book offers a detailed explanation of the specific parts in upcoming chapters, but rather more context for the broader concepts coming up.

Chapter Two, or at least a chapter that's very high up in the hierarchy of a nonfiction book, is often an assessment or a "taking stock" chapter, particularly for books that are somewhat prescriptive. In other words, if your nonfiction book is meant to solve a problem (which many nonfiction books are), you might want to put the onus on the reader to see themselves in the book. Chapter Two is very often a "looking inward" type of chapter for the reader where they can think about their pain points and what they want to try to get out of the book. Oftentimes these chapters include really specific assessments or quizzes. If that's not your style or you don't want to include something that prescriptive, that that's fine too.

Chapter Three is where the rubber meets the road, and the substantive chapters kick off. When developing an initial TOC for the proposal, think of this as the first "main idea" chapter built around your book's primary thesis. If you remember from any composition classes you took in high school or college, your main concept of an essay (or a book in your case) should have at least three to five claims to back up your primary concept. You've already done some of the work here when you brainstormed your idea and developed those claims. Now, they can become your chapters.

No matter how many "meaty" chapters you add to the TOC, be sure to include a final chapter that brings it all together and sends the reader forth with what they have learned. What do I mean by that? I mean that the final chapter is not necessarily a summary of the entire book, but rather it's a place for all of those ideas to generate together and culminate into a big, final takeaway for the reader. Oftentimes, these final chapters also have a "go out and set the world on fire" kind of tone to them because it's natural to want the reader to end their book-reading experience with a feeling of empowerment. As a subject-matter expert, you've shared your knowledge, so of course you hope the reader takes something from your book to go apply it to their life. Many times, your final chapter will serve that purpose.

Finally, when you're crafting the table of contents for the proposal, be sure to include any extra goodies that you think will bring value to the reader for your book. These value-adds are usually included in appendices. Say you've got forms or charts or worksheets that don't necessarily fit into the narrative flow of the rest of the book. You can use them as bonus content at the end or as online content accessible with a QR code. It's also appropriate to include any kind of related sales information whether you're trying to link your book to a course or your broader business—as long as it does not detract from the editorial quality of your content. In other words, include mention of related products or services—but don't overdo it. Other common backmatter items to include are your About the Author page and Acknowledgments.

CHAPTER SUMMARIES

Now that you've built out a full table of contents, it's time to dig into describing each individual chapter for your proposal reader. When we talk about the landscape of what a book proposal looks like, the chapter overviews serve as "mini proposals" or overviews for each individual chapter. These are like mini elevator pitches, so they have to do a lot of things. Chapter summaries should:

- Entice the reader about what's in that chapter by hooking the reader with valuable and compelling descriptions.
- Summarize what is in each chapter with rich detail and valuable takeaways.
- Offer color and delight with anecdotal information and interesting tidbits.

That's a lot of heavy lifting—and these aren't even full chapters! Chapter overviews are typically one to two good, strong paragraphs that provide a useful snapshot so the reader has a solid conceptual vision of your book. Now, if you have a very complicated topic you can go a little bit longer on these chapter overviews, but I certainly wouldn't do more than half a page to 3/4 of a page. If you have a lot of chapters (say, more than 10), it's vital to summarize the chapter content and keep your eye on the ball by not getting overly descriptive. You have a lot of ground to cover, so keep your narrative language tight. Don't go too off the rails. Think of the chapter summaries as mini stand-alone sections. If you have any notable sources, data points, or stats that are pertinent to the tone and quality of that chapter, then you will want to include them. For example, if your Chapter One is indeed your survey course chapter and you're making the case for your topic, consider including a couple of pertinent statistics that back up the chapter concept. Or, if you've got a chapter that's more of an activity based chapter where you're having the reader complete worksheets or take some quizzes or self-assessments, be specific in your summary and list out what those activities are here. Keep in mind that you're writing to entice the reader, you want them to buy your project or partner with you in some way. So your summaries shouldn't be droll, nor speculative. They should be reflective of the content so the decision maker reading your proposal can have an accurate picture of your book's content.

THE SAMPLE CHAPTER

Perhaps the most daunting part of the book proposal for many authors is the sample chapter. This is a fully realized chapter that you are presenting—not an outline or summary. A real, fleshed-out chapter. Many authors feel a great deal of pressure to write a "perfect" sample chapter, thinking that it will be the one thing that makes or breaks their proposal. While it's perfectly normal to feel this way, please release some of the pressure you feel. A sample chapter isn't your only shot to impress a decision maker. Rather, think of it as a window into the project for the reader. All of the other sections of your proposal are windows, too. Does a house just have a single window? No—it has several to let in the light. This particular window shines a sliver of light on your project—not the whole sun.

How do you select a sample chapter to showcase your writing skills and provide that window for your reader? First of all, the chapter you choose should not be Chapter One. Why? Chapter one is so often a general overview or survey course to your topic that it doesn't really get into the deep work of concept like the rest of your book does. And it doesn't necessarily showcase your skill as a writer because it can be too rudimentary.

The sample chapter you *do* write should be a strong representative of your concept or your thesis—it should be a "meaty" chapter. Most folks tend to choose something from the middle of the book where they're diving into the topic area and they can showcase some specific writing or conceptual skills. Your sample chapter should also be one that showcases your expertise. In other words, maybe you have a chapter that's mostly theory based, but you don't include any case studies or assessments. Okay, then let's avoid that chapter for this exercise. Instead, choose a chapter that shows a little bit of all that you're bringing to the table: narrative, anecdotes, examples, data, etc. So if you've got a more prescriptive, hands-on book, choose a chapter that has an activity for the reader, worksheets, or a great takeaway.

However, perhaps you're not doing a book that is like that at all. Maybe you're writing something that's narrative nonfiction, memoir, a cookbook, or even a how-to craft book. If that's you, then select a chapter that really speaks to the heart of your topic and showcases the best approach to that topic for your voice.

The sample chapter should also center the reader's experience. Choosing one that includes something more hands-on, as I mentioned earlier, is a really good way to do that. If you've got those kinds of chapters, give one a try as your sample chapter and see how you like it. Letting the reader see themselves **in** the text by including them in an active role really goes a long way toward humanizing your approach.

If you've got chapters that have firm takeaways for the reader and are a little less theory-based or are more practical and/or prescriptive, they might also be great choices for a sample chapter. While actionable takeaways are important, not every nonfiction book has firm "takeaways" at the end of each chapter. However, every chapter should provide something for the reader that they can apply to their own life, so find one within your TOC that really speaks to the reader and centers them on the experience. Show them the problem you're trying to fix and how you're going to fix it.

Finally, make it fun! What's your favorite chapter in your TOC? What do you love to write about? What sets your writer's heart on fire? I guarantee if you choose a chapter that you enjoyed writing or developing, someone's going to enjoy reading it because your enthusiasm and your expertise can form a massive powerhouse together that draws your reader in.

THE OVERVIEW

The last first element of the "Are you a good writer?" part of the proposal is the overview. Now, including this last may seem a bit odd, as the overview is typically the first section of a book proposal. That's true—it is. But I am covering it last here because ideally, it's the last element of the proposal you should write so it best captures all that is in the proposal.

The overview is exactly what it sounds like—it's an overview of your proposal. If you are business-minded, think of it as you would an executive summary. The overview provides not only a survey of all the sections in the proposal, but a summary and analysis of the project as a whole.

The overview has to do a few things:

- **It entices your reader with a hook.** By a hook, I mean that the overview draws your reader in with something that's different, interesting, and compelling. You can do that in a lot of different ways. For example, maybe you've got a really great anecdote to tell about your book, your topic, or what made you write the book. Maybe it's an anecdote about someone you interviewed for your book and it's a unique, out-of-the-box, rich story with good detail. A strong hook makes people want to read more.

- **It has to introduce your main concept, idea, or thesis.** This is the big takeaway from your book. If you had to tell me in one sentence what your book is about, what would it be? That's what you can explain and expand on here in the overview.
- **It introduces you as the subject-matter expert.** The overview is the first thing your reader will skim over before diving into the full proposal. Not only do they want to know what your book concept is about, they want to know why **you** are the best person to write it. Since the overview is finite (usually a page or two), you don't have room to say everything you want to say about yourself in relation to the project. Instead, you weave in your "highlight reel" and mention the most relevant parts of your relative experience.
- **It showcases the most vital parts of your marketing platform and plan.** This goal goes hand in hand with including your author bona fides. Remember: Your goal is to pitch the concept **and** you as the expert. So it's worth weaving in some of the finer points of both your current author platform and offer a few examples of what your marketing plan will accomplish.

Finally, and perhaps most importantly, the overview tells the story of the book's "why." Why does this book matter? Why is it needed right now? Why are you the right person to write it? All of these things are covered in the overview in one to two pages so that you can introduce the editor or the agent or other stakeholder to the overall concept of this book before they dive into the specific details of the rest of your book proposal.

Now that you have a better understanding of the "Are you a good writer?" part of the proposal, let's get started on creating a couple of the elements that speak to that. But first, take some time to map out a tentative table of contents, then get started on drafting your overview.

Activity 6A
WRITE A TABLE OF CONTENTS

Use this space to map out your TOC. Keep in mind that there is no one perfect way to craft your table of contents, and structure may vary based on your topic area and approach.

1. Foreword

....
....
....
....
....

2. Introduction

....
....
....
....
....

3. "Survey course" chapter

....
....
....
....
....

4. "Assessment" chapter

....
....
....
....
....

5. "Main course" chapters

....
....
....
....
....
....
....
....
....
....
....
....
....
....
....
....
....
....

6. "Go forth and conquer" chapter

....
....
....
....
....

7. The extra goodies (appendix, bonus content, etc.)

....
....
....
....
....

Activity 6B
WRITE THE OVERVIEW

Your overview should reflect your final book concept, touch on the existing market for the book, and provide a summary of the primary book content. Your overview should be approximately 1-2 pages long.

1. How will you to draw in the reader?

2. Introduction of book concept/main thesis

3. Book summary

4. Evidence points for the book's need/Position in the market:

....
....
....
....
....
....

5. Description of the book's "why"

....
....
....
....
....
....

6. Additional information

....
....
....
....
....
....
....
....
....
....
....
....
....
....
....
....

Write the Book Proposal, Part 2: Focus on the Marketing

NOW THAT YOU HAVE the "Are You a Good Writer?" portion of the proposal handled, it's time to dig into the "Are You a Good Marketer?" section. This part of the proposal is often a bigger challenge for emerging authors—especially if they do not typically view themselves as marketing savvy. Many of the authors with whom I work are entrepreneurs and actively working in the small business space, so they often have marketing tools already in place for their business and brand. However, many others work in content areas that don't naturally lend themselves to the benefits of traditional marketing channels—or so they think. In today's high-touch, highly connected book marketing landscape, the opportunities to promote your book and brand are endless. Finding those opportunities is all about getting creative and reaching potential readers where they are, whether that's on social media, at an industry conference, at your local farmer's market, or even in an enthusiast forum. Your readers are there—you just have to reach them using your expertise and content. Remember: Publishing is a business. We don't just publish books we love—we also publish books that make money for the publisher and hopefully for the author as well. That is why the marketing portion of your proposal is valuable to your publishing journey—and anyone with whom you work. Let's dive into the sections you'll need to make your marketing shine.

ANALYZE THE MARKET FOR YOUR BOOK

Next, you'll explore the market for your book and prepare a market analysis, which you first learned about in Step 5. Start by talking about the current market landscape for your project. Here, you explore the need for your topic and your particular niche. You want to tell a compelling, data-driven story about your book and why it's worth publishing. You'll also circle back to how your book is different and has a niche that can be maximized for sales potential.

When you're doing a market analysis, you're doing a couple of things. The first is that you're explaining your audience profile—in other words, who is going to read this book. Remember the reader avatars you created earlier? This is where you will refer to them and discuss them in the context of marketing and selling your book. Here, you'll take those reader avatars and include some related demographics about them so your reader can quantify the market for your idea.

The market analysis should also identify the need in the marketplace of ideas for your book's topic. In other words, who's going to read it and why. When you're discussing that market landscape, it's important that you talk about the "why" in quantifiable terms. You can't just say, "Everyone needs my book; it's great!" Leave that sort of puffery out and leave those subjective words behind. Words and phrases like "great," or "useful," or "has heart" are laudatory things to say about your book, but that doesn't help sell your book to someone who reads proposals every single day. Instead, you need to make a case for your book by showing data and anecdotal evidence to demonstrate that the market needs your unique point of view. To do that, use statistics, studies, and reports to make your case. Keep in mind this is the section about market analysis so it's really important first that you highlight what the market is for your book, the need for it, and who might be potential readers for it. This is also where you can contextualize your project by talking about the topic in general. For example, in the post-pandemic world, you might want to write a book about a related topic like coworking, how working has changed, or how it's different now. Would this be a book that could have been written a few years ago? Possibly, but it wouldn't have had the timely punch that it does today. So, use stats, studies, and reports to help make that case and then identify specific market areas of interest for your book. By specific market areas, I mean that you can use some broad strokes to describe who might be interested in reading your book, including:

- Enthusiasts or students of your topic
- Professionals
- Members of related associations and organizations
- Special-interest groups
- Social media groups and followers
- Readers interested in adjacent topic areas
- Readers affected by events that take place in your content area

Let's look at an example of a potential audience from a special interest group. Say you're writing a parenting book and it's very specifically about how to get toddlers to go to bed. You could go in a lot of directions when describing this market. You can't just say that parents generally will read this book. Rather, focus on describing a specific group like parents of toddlers who struggle with bedtime. Offer some statistics on how many parents say they have toddlers who struggle with bedtime. Then you could go in even deeper and talk about different associations or groups or even social media outreach groups that focus on that topic.

Next, dive into identifying your audience by pulling some stats and weaving in even more demographic information to highlight who your potential readers are. These demographics can talk about broader-stroke approaches to market interest levels. Some demographics of your potential audience could include:

- Age
- Gender
- Political affiliation
- Education

- Family status
- Religious affiliation
- Income level

You can also discuss relevant secondary audience members (remember your secondary and lower-tier reader avatars here). Going back to our example of parents of toddlers who have a hard time going to bed, perhaps a related secondary audience here would be teachers and preschool or daycare providers who want to help parents bridge that gap with tools they can use during the day to better position children for bedtime at night. Another related or secondary audience for that topic might be pediatricians, social workers, psychologists, or psychiatrists who work with families who are dealing with these issues. As you can see, once you start digging in deeper to the potential market for your book, you'll find many layers.

WRITE THE COMPETITIVE ANALYSIS

Remember the competitive research you did in Step 4? This is when you get to use it! Writing a competitive analysis is an important part of the proposal because you are helping your reader understand where your book fits into the current publishing landscape. This is important information for them to have (especially if you are approaching a traditional publisher) because a book that has a unique angle is one that will stand out to potential customers.

When you do a competitive analysis, you highlight how your book is better or different from others like it on the shelf. This is your opportunity to show that the concept you are selling here is better, different, or unique in some way than the books that are already out in the world.

It's not enough to say, "My book is better because I think so." Tell your readers why and give them at least one to two nuggets of true differentiation between your book and your competitors' book.

To create your competitive title list, refer back to your initial competitive research and choose 5-7 comp titles to include in this section. Each competitive book you list should include the following information:

- Title
- Author
- Publication year
- Price
- Publisher
- Page count
- Trim size
- Brief summary (one paragraph)
- Analysis of the book's strengths and weaknesses
- How your book is better or different

These data points are useful not only to the decision maker reading your proposal, but to you as well. Exploring your competition helps you strengthen your vision for the project so when it comes time to market it in real-world situations, you know how to position it against the competition.

Your book could be a new take on a classic topic, or it could be a wildly divergent viewpoint from the norm. Perhaps is an unexplored niche entirely. For example, there are lots of books out there about women's rhetoric and feminist rhetoric, especially in the academic space. Let's say that you have a book about a specific type of women's studies. Maybe it's women's rhetoric in letters or women's rhetoric in letters from a certain time period. Those are niches that you could position as new or updated territory. Your book may be different in such a way because it includes updated material or research that's completely new to your topic area. Perhaps you offer a more robust, reader-centric approach to a topic that's typically viewed as more theoretical.

Maybe your topic has been widely written about, but no one has really applied it to everyday life. An example of this might be the topic of scrum master training. Let's say that I'm an editor who wants to acquire a book about scrum master training. I don't just want readers to learn about how to be a scrum master, I want them to know what it takes to pass the certification test to get a high-level job in that field. So, as an editor, I would be looking for books that focus on that as opposed to just a general content piece about what a scrum master does.

You can also differentiate your book by mentioning any bonus content you plan to include. Perhaps your book is directly connected to a course or an online seminar. You can also differentiate yourself by showing the strength of your existing author platform as it relates to your competitors' platforms.

No matter what titles you use in your competitive analysis, remember to cover these three main points for each entry:

- Pertinent book information
- Summary of the competitive title
- How your book is different

These three elements of each entry will help you structure the competitive analysis and keep it well organized.

DESCRIBE YOUR CURRENT BRAND PLATFORM

The next part of the proposal is your author platform. Again, your author platform is all about what you already have in your wheelhouse in terms of marketing and support—not what you aspire to do. You want to include real numbers and not aspirational ones. For example, when you describe your social media numbers, your potential publishing partners will want to know your actual follower count, not what you hope will be in six months. When it comes to your website, be extremely specific about what the web traffic is for it.

Keep in mind that this can and should be a "kitchen sink" list of your current brand platform. Include anything that might possibly be a way for you to market your book. Here are a few examples of what you can include in your author platform section:

- **Web presence.** Discuss all the information you have about your website, including URL, web traffic numbers, and SEO information.
- **Content ecosystem.** This is anything content-related that you create. This could be blogs, articles, LinkedIn posts, newsletters,

print media, courses, mini books or ancillary material, and posts on sites like Medium or Substack (don't forget to include the number of subscribers!).

- **E-mail list.** If you have a dedicated e-mail list either for your business or brand, include information about how many e-mails are on it and the frequency with which you contact them.
- **Social media.** Your potential editor or publishing partner wants to know your follower count on every possible platform: Facebook, X, Instagram, LinkedIn, and Pinterest.
- **Event outreach.** Do you do events and/or speak to people at conferences, conventions, and seminars? These can be virtual or in person. Either way, your potential editor wants to know about them including the names of the events, attendance numbers, and the topics about which you speak.
- **Memberships or associations.** List them all. This can even include alumni associations or groups that you're a part of in your community. It doesn't just have to be related to your topic. Any group that you are involved with is a group where your book can be marketed.
- **Confirmed connections or endorsements.** This group includes anyone who is a subject-matter expert themselves or somehow associated with your topic who can provide a testimonial for your book. These people should have some kind of name recognition within your topic area space.

These are the primary examples of what to include in the brand platform section. That said, every author is different and comes with a varied background, so your results may vary. My advice is to list anything in your current platform that could be a place to market your book project.

CREATE A VALUABLE MARKETING PLAN

Next up is the marketing plan—it's what you are going to do to sell the book. A marketing plan differs from your author platform. Remember: The platform is what you already have in place in terms of how you market yourself and what your outreach looks like. The marketing plan is where the rubber hits the road in that it is how you will apply that existing author platform to market and sell your book. Again—this should be realistic, not aspirational.

Your marketing plan should be actionable, too. In other words, it should be something that you can put into motion fairly easily or quickly by you or by a team that you're going to hire. A lot of authors hire outside PR firms to help them make marketing plans come to fruition, while others take a purely grassroots approach and do most of the marketing outreach themselves.

Here are a few examples of what you can include in a marketing plan:

- **Specific information about planned web outreach connected to your already existing brand.** This can be either a personal or corporate website. By that, I mean if you're already known for speaking on a topic and you likely already have a website that details that, you've written other books, or maybe you teach courses, you probably have a branded website that already speaks to all of those other verticals. If not, perhaps you have a corporate website that you can link yourself to whether it's for your business or for a business in which you have a high-profile role that would be willing to let you also market your book.
- **Social strategy.** We talked already about providing clear and compelling detail about what your social media outreach already is in the author platform section. Now it's time to talk about what you're going to do with it. Be specific and describe how you will leverage your social media presence to market your book. You might even want to include a brief editorial calendar saying how you're going to roll out posts about the book launch. Talk a little bit about any ad spend that you might be willing to do for social media ads on Facebook, TikTok, or Instagram or even paid advertising on LinkedIn. Mention any live videos that you're going to include in your outreach. Discuss how you plan to incorporate purchasing links into any of your posts. In other words, are you going to include links for retailers so followers can buy your book? Are you going to sell some books direct

through your website too? All the social strategy in the world doesn't mean anything if your readers don't know how to go out and buy the book.

- **E-mail strategy.** Even if you don't have a huge e-mail list, this is a good place to talk about your specific plans to grow it so you can market your book directly to your dedicated followers. Talk about what you can put in place today before your book even comes out and how you're going to grow that e-mail list. Maybe you already have a really great e-mail list in place. If so, this is the time to map out ways you'll reach people about the book launch, get people excited for the book, and incorporate a buying or selling strategy.

- **Special offers.** Mention any special offers or purchase incentives you plan to offer to readers. For example, perhaps you would like to focus on corporate buys for your book. Perhaps you want to offer incentives for anyone who buys 1 to 25 books, so you offer some kind of free lead generation piece like a white paper. For people who buy 100 books or more, you could offer a free online seminar or free coaching session. There are lots of different ways to incentivize people and companies to buy larger quantities of books. So, think a little bit about what you might be able to offer at low cost to you that can help you sell more books.

- **Media appearances that you can realistically schedule.** This can be anything from television appearances to podcast interviews. Provide a list of potential appearances you are confident you can get on the calendar.

- **Event and association outreach.** What kind of speaking is on the radar for you in the coming year? Are you going to be doing virtual events? Will you be doing live events or appearances linked to an association or organization related to your topic area? If you do corporate speaking, conference keynotes, or provide a special online seminar or seminar for such events, those are people to reach out to about purchasing back-of-room copies of your book for event attendees. If these groups won't make a bulk purchase, see if they will allow you to hand-sell copies after your speaking engagement.

- **Testimonials.** This is the time to call in favors and list people you ***know*** will sing your praises and help sell your book. Give some background about who these people are and how you plan to maximize their reach. Maybe these people will post for you on LinkedIn, give you a testimonial, or even send something out to their own e-mail list. There are so many ways that you can maximize your personal connections.

The key to creating a valuable and actionable marketing plan is to leverage your existing author platform to the best of your ability. You won't necessarily have every marketing element in tip-top shape, and that's OK. Focus in on those major pieces that apply to you. For example, not everybody is highly engaged and active on social media. Or maybe you don't have an e-mail list. In such cases, map out realistic plans to grow in those areas and go HAM on the marketing elements you **do** have working for you.

It's time to continue building your proposal. Next, let's work on two activities that I think will really help you wrap your brain around what it takes to put these marketing pieces together. First, **Activity 7A** will help you create your market analysis. Remember, the marketing analysis is where you're talking about the broader market for the book and how your book might fit into the content landscape. Next, in **Activity 7B**, you'll create your marketing plan using all of the pieces that we just discussed like social media, event outreach, and more.

Activity 7A
WRITE A MARKETING ANALYSIS

Use this worksheet to draft your marketing analysis. Ideally, this section of the proposal is 1-2 pages long.

1. Primary market size

....
....
....

2. Secondary market size

....
....
....

3. What is the "why" for *this* book for *this* market

....
....
....
....
....
....
....
....

4. Describe how this book's niche will speak to the market

....
....
....
....
....
....
....
....

5. Specific market areas of interest (associations, industries, interests)

....

....

....

....

....

....

....

....

....

6. Audience demographics

....

....

....

....

....

....

....

....

....

7. Ideal reader avatar

....

....

....

....

....

....

....

....

....

Activity 7B
CREATE YOUR MARKETING PLAN

Use this worksheet to draft your marketing plan. Use the Marketing Analysis to brainstorm specific actions you can take to market your book. Ideally, this section of the proposal is 2-4 pages long.

1. Online/websites

....
....
....
....
....

2. Social media

....
....
....
....
....

3. E-mail lists

....
....
....
....
....
....

4. Corporate/speaking/events

....
....
....
....
....

5. Media appearances/interviews/podcasts

6. Outreach by personal contacts

7. Paid outreach and PR

STEP 8

Create the Book Proposal Package

NOW THAT YOU HAVE CREATED all the parts of your book proposal, it's time to put everything together. I like to think of your book proposal package as a living document, one that you can change and update over time to suit your needs. In the early days of your publishing journey, you'll most likely use this proposal package to pitch your book to agents, editors, or potential business partners. But I would also encourage you to look at it as a living business plan for your book project. I've mentioned that before here, but it bears repeating. Keep in mind that you are the boss of your book project, and having a proposal package to refer back to often and update as needed helps you keep fresh all of the ideas that you want to use as the project progresses. In this chapter, we'll talk about customizing your query letter, which is an important part of the pitching process, and some final steps you'll want to take when assembling your book proposal package. Let's go!

CUSTOMIZE THE QUERY

It's time to think about what your initial outreach to potential publishers or business partners will be like. This is your book query. When you have a book proposal ready to present, you don't just send it out to everyone who you think might be interested. Instead, you float a little balloon out there to see if anyone takes it. That's your query letter—also known as a pitch.

A pitch does a few things for you, but most importantly it tees up your proposal. It is typically a one-page letter that you write to editors and agents to pique their interest so you can determine if they want to see that full book proposal and talk to you about publishing your book. Think of it as the cover letter for your book project that operates like a hook or a tease to the decision makers to make them want more. The pitch (if it works) makes them want to learn all about your book project, so you've really got to offer them a great hook to entice them. You can't just say, "Here's my book. Here's who I am. I hope you read it."

Instead, you need to draw them in with something that's compelling and unique that makes them see this is something a little bit out of the ordinary from its competitors. The pitch should be short and to the point with a hook, then an explanation of what your book is and why you're the best person to write it. You really have to do three things here you have to:

1. **Hook your reader with something unique like an interesting story, anecdote, or a quote from a thought leader in your space who's read your book and liked it.** This hook should be something to make them stop and think, "Oh! This sounds intriguing. I'm going to read more."
2. **Explain what your book is in a meaty paragraph.** Consider dropping in a couple of statistics about the market for your book or its potential readership so that you can make a case for why the book is important, why it matters, or why it's different.
3. **Finally, you want to say something about you and why you're the right person to write this book.** Tap into your bona fides as the subject-matter expert and note a few highlights of your connection to and influence on the topic.

You can accomplish writing a solid pitch in one page or in a concise e-mail. Think of your pitch in terms of three primary paragraphs based on the three points I just mentioned. This is your structure. Then of course you want to close it out with a with a brief paragraph thanking them for their time and offering to show them the full proposal if they are interested.

Remember: Your pitch isn't a brain dump about your book project. Rather, it's an invitation to learn more. It should be short, sweet, and to the point. Think about pitching your book project as you might think about job hunting. When you go out to find a new job and you're out there with a million other people who also want a job in your field, what sets you apart from the competition and makes potential employers want to learn more about you? Your cover letter. That is how your pitch operates, too. It entices your reader to dig more deeply into who you are as a subject-matter expert so they want to read your full proposal.

ASSEMBLE THE BOOK PROPOSAL

Once you have the pitch written and all of the elements of the proposal written, it's time to assemble the pieces of your proposal so you are ready to send it out to those who express interest in seeing more.

To put it all together, you first need to think about what your primary proposal focus will be. There are a couple of different ways to assemble a proposal depending on what you want to focus your reader on. Do you want them to focus more on your writing ability? Perhaps your author platform and your marketing plan are a little on the light side and you want to highlight your writing chops to make sure the editor or agent are pulled in by your skill. Maybe you have an exceptionally strong author platform and marketing plan, and you want that to be the first thing they read. Let's explore what those two different iterations look like.

- **Writing Focus.** If you want the writing to be the focus of the reader's attention, then assemble the components of your proposal like this:

  - Title page
  - Overview
  - Table of contents

- Chapter summaries
- Sample chapter
- Market analysis
- Competitive analysis
- Author bio and platform
- Marketing plan

- **Marketing Focus.** If you want to highlight the marketing first and have that be what grabs your readers attention your version would look like this:

  - Title page
  - Overview
  - Market analysis
  - Competitive analysis
  - Author bio and platform
  - Marketing plan
  - Table of contents
  - Chapter summaries
  - Sample chapter

To determine which version is better for you, focus on what sections are strongest. If a particular section knocks it out of the park in terms of persuasive information, lead with it. However, if your topic area is something that you're either stepping into as an emerging writer or you don't have what you think is a firm platform just yet, focus on the writing piece.

I would also recommend you do the "writing focus" version if your book is deeply personal like narrative nonfiction or memoir.

Walk Away

Once you've assembled everything, it's time to give it a rest. In other words, you need to take some time away from your proposal. Give yourself room to breathe. Give the proposal room to breathe. Don't just write your proposal and then run off and send it to everybody every agent and editor that you want to pitch to. Instead, step away from it for a while.

Doing this gives your brain and your eyes time to refresh. Have you ever worked on something and then you came back a couple of days later and found a lot of typos? Or maybe you found some wording or phrasing that was off, or you found transitions that didn't really work but you didn't notice those things in the moment? That's what time away gives you. Stepping away from your proposal for a few days gives you some perspective on your writing.

If you're on a tight timeline to get that proposal out, take at least a couple of days to step away from it and then come back to it and look at it with fresh eyes. Two weeks, however, is even better. If you have a longer lead time, I would recommend building this in. Really walk away from it, forget about it entirely, go do other things, and then come back to it.

You can use this time to your advantage and turn your brain on to another part of this process, which is researching agents, editors, and potential publishing partners. We already covered this a bit earlier, but it's worth mentioning here because it's a good way to stay engaged and active with your project while you let the proposal "marinate" before you dive back in to do a final edit on it.

Remember: Not every agent is going to represent the kind of book that you're writing nor is every editor publishing it. So, use this time to do that part of your research to determine what agents and editors are appropriate for you to pitch. Also look into what their submission guidelines are so that you know what you need to meet their requirements.

You can also use this time to refine your pitch or query letter so you can make sure that it really fits the feel of the proposal and that you're saying everything you want to say.

Self-Editing

When you do come back to your proposal, it's time to do some self-editing. An editing process I have used and taught for years is a simple, guided way to review your writing that you can apply to just about any project. It's called "HOCs and LOCs."

HOCs and LOCs stand for higher-order concerns and lower-order concerns. Basically, this means that you do a couple of reads of your work, with the first read focused on major concerns, and the second read focused on more finite issues. As you self-edit your proposal, start by reading for your higher-order concerns (HOCs). These are big-picture items like:

- Clarity
- Organization
- Breadth and depth of the information
- Ease of navigation for the reader

Does everything make sense? Do you have everything in the order that you want it to be in? Are there good transitions between paragraphs? All of these things are higher-order concerns that are focused on the reader experience. For example, can the reader navigate your writing to best understand your main points?

After that, read for lower-order concerns (LOCs). These are more finite editorial items like:

- Sentence structure
- Paragraph-level transitions
- General syntax
- Grammar and punctuation

Once you've gone through your HOCs and LOCs, it's time to do a final grammar check. We all have grammar ticks that we don't notice while we are writing. Some people have a big problem with writing in parallel structure. Some people misuse words, while others have issues with tense usage. There are all kinds of things we all do grammar-wise that we know we shouldn't, so do your best to find out what those things are that you do and do a final grammar check for yourself. Of course, any kind of writing software that you use, whether it's Microsoft Word or Google Docs, has a spell check and grammar check function. I would recommend running those, but remember they're not infallible and they don't always catch everything. So, make sure you go through it and read it carefully to make sure that everything is spelled correctly and that your grammar looks great. Also check your work for redundancy. Are you repeating yourself? Granted, there are some things in your proposal that do tend to overlap a little bit, so some redundancy is natural. for example, some of the stats that you use in your overview to make the case for your idea might pop up again in your marketing analysis. That's OK but try not to use the exact same language to convey those data points. Mix up your language a bit.

Get Feedback

Finally, once you're done with self-editing, get yourself an outside reader who is not emotionally invested in your success. You know what I'm going to say next: That means family. Now, family is great. Friends are great. But they want you to succeed and sometimes they have a really hard time telling you that something needs work. So, try to find yourself an outside reader, perhaps someone who's a fellow subject matter expert who can read your proposal with clarity, confidence, and objectivity. A reader who gives your work the critical care it deserves and who can relay useful feedback to you is much more valuable to your process that someone who can only provide you with empty kudos.

MAKE THE PITCH

Once you've determined if you're going to pitch to agents, editors, or potential publishing partners, it's time to send out your pitch. It's important to have a process so you don't just send out query letters willy nilly. You want to be highly organized throughout this process.

First, confirm the submission guidelines for both agents and publishers. These stakeholders typically include this information right on their websites.

They will also tell you how to do present a pitch or query letter and how they like to receive them. Most people want to receive them via e-mail, and there's usually a dedicated e-mail address just for the purpose of gathering pitches. Many agents and editors also take part in different kinds of pitch competitions. They may also have certain times a year when they are closed to queries and certain times when they're open to queries. Be sure you check that out, so you know what they expect.

Once you confirm those submission guidelines, follow them. If you cannot follow the directions laid out by a potential agent or editor, that's a red flag to them. Everyone feels like their book is the most important book in the world, and to you it is, but keep in mind that these people review thousands of query letters each year. They are constantly barraged by people who want to publish a book too, so for you to stand out not only does your proposal have to sing and be perfect, you need to follow the instructions set forth by the agent or the publisher.

You can also tweak your pitch letter for each agent or publisher. Keep in mind that publishing professionals are not a monolith. Everyone from agents to hybrid publishers has different guidelines that we want to follow, and we have different publishing interests. So, think hard about how you can tweak it a little bit to fit that particular agent or publisher. For example, you might mention a specific related project that they've published or represented. You might want to mention any special connections that you have to them. Perhaps you have a friend or a colleague whom they published. It's fine to have a name drop here, so tweak your pitch letter and make it special for each one.

Follow Up

I hate to tell you this, but you'll have to engage in a practice called "hurry up and wait." Editors and agents are looking at hundreds of pitches and proposals all the time, every single month. It takes a while to get through all of them, so don't push or expect an immediate response. You're going to have to be very, very patient and follow up when necessary. For example, if an agent or an editor has on their website that they respond to queries within a certain amount of time and you haven't heard anything back in that certain amount of time, it is acceptable at that point to shoot them a quick follow up e-mail just to ask where they are in the process. I wouldn't do this early. At most publishing houses, it can take up to a few months before you hear any feedback. So don't e-mail them in two days and say, "Did you read my proposal?" or, "Did you read my query letter?" Give agents, editors, and publishing partners plenty of time. Folks are really busy in our business, so have a heart and be OK with being patient.

Now that we've talked a little bit about the pitch, let's go ahead and map out what that query or elevator pitch might look like. In **Activity 8**, I've created a space where you can think about it, brainstorm your ideal language, and create your own perfect pitch.

Activity 8
CREATE YOUR PITCH/QUERY

1. **Hook: How will you draw in the reader?** Use an anecdote, jaw-dropping statistic, or fact to capture their attention.

2. **Summary of concept:** Provide a simple summary of your book's main idea, keeping it simple and high-level.

3. **Why is the idea important? Why does it matter to a general readership? Why would someone buy your book?** Use some stats/info to make a case for the size of your audience.

4. **Why are you the best person to write about it?** This is where you make your credentials shine.

5. **The Closer:** Close it out with information on requesting a full proposal, contact info, and thanks.

Paragraph 1: The Hook

....

....

....

....

....

....

....

....

....

....

....

....

....

....

....

....

Paragraph 2: The Summary

Paragraph 3: The "Why"

Paragraph 4: The "Why Me"

....
....
....
....
....
....
....
....
....
....
....
....
....
....
....

Paragraph 5: The Closer

....
....
....
....
....
....
....
....
....
....
....
....
....
....
....
....

STEP 9

Determine Your Path

SO FAR, your publishing journey has taken you through several phases, from developing your original book concept to writing a full proposal that you can use as a business plan for your book no matter what path you take. You have laid the groundwork for what comes next, which is... Well, what, exactly? Have you discovered that being the CEO of your book is what you want, so self-publishing is the route you want to go? Or perhaps you want the distribution and marketing support of a more traditional publisher, but you also want some creative control and higher royalties with a hybrid publisher. After going through the process of doing the competitive research and writing a full proposal, maybe you want to go all in with an agent or pitch to a traditional publishing house. As you know by now, the possibilities are endless. What matters most, though, is what YOU want to do to achieve your publishing goals. What path works best for you can only be determined by one person—you. That's what we'll unpack in this chapter—determining the path you want to take on your publishing journey.

KNOW WHAT YOU WANT

When you are determining the path that you take with your publishing project, it's important to honor yourself first. Honor who you are and what you want out of this process. It's extremely easy for first-time authors to fall into the trap of doing what other people tell them to do or following a path that someone else suggests may not necessarily be right for them. I would urge you to reject the opinions of the masses when it comes to what suits you and your project best. This isn't to say that you shouldn't accept advice from people who have either been in your shoes or who have professional expertise in publishing. But crowdsourcing every idea related to your project will not serve you well in the long run. I always tell authors to keep in mind that they likely have a lot of well-meaning people in their corner who want them to succeed in their publishing journey. Whether that's friends, family members, fellow authors, or colleagues, people want what is best for you most of the time. That doesn't, however, mean that they have educated opinions about publishing and how it works. You have done the legwork so far in this process and done a lot of research. You have already done the hard intellectual parts of this process. Now, it's time for you to look within and do some emotional work as well. Ask yourself what you really want here. You can do that by first exploring your goals.

Set Goals

What do you want to achieve with your book project? We talked a little bit about this at the beginning of the book, but I'd like to revisit it with you. Are your goals to help further an existing business? Do you want to use your book as a calling card? Perhaps you already have an existing content ecosystem and are eager to include a new vertical through a book. Or maybe you just have a burning desire to write about your area of expertise and you don't really know where to go with it yet. That's OK too!

Take a few moments to jot down some of your primary and secondary goals for your book project. If you are familiar with smart goals, use that as a template for mapping this out. Smart goals are:

Specific   Measurable   Achievable   Relevant   Time-bound

In other words, your goals should not just be pie-in-the-sky ideas but specific enough that you can wrap your brain around what they would look like if you moved forward with achieving them. Let's use an example here. Say that I am a small business consultant, and I am writing a book about how to manage a team. I already do a lot of speaking and run masterminds as a part of my business. I have an existing content ecosystem with a blog, social media presence, and a website. When thinking about what I want out of a book project, here is what my smart goals would look like:

- **Specific:** I want to write a book about managing small teams so that I can use it as a part of my mastermind course and sell it at speaking events.
- **Measurable:** I want to sell at least 5000 copies, 2000 of which will be sold direct-to-consumer so I can retain a higher profit margin.
- **Achievable:** I'm going to use some of my existing content to write the book and keep it at a manageable page count of under 200 pages.
- **Relevant:** I will be using this book as a value-added offering for my mastermind, my courses, and at speaking events that are geared toward those who manage small teams.
- **Time-bound:** I would like to publish this book within the next 18 months.

In this example, you can see that the author has set some goals that are both manageable and relevant to their particular area of expertise. Let's look at a second example, but this time the authors area of expertise is in an enthusiast content area as opposed to a more business-focused subject matter. Let's say I am a chef who wants to write a cookbook to promote my restaurant. Here are what my goals would look like:

- **Specific:** I want to write a book about regional cuisine from my area.
- **Measurable:** I want to be able to sell my cookbook at my restaurant as well as at major online retailers.

- **Achievable:** I'm going to tap into my treasure trove of recipes and anecdotal stories from my life as a chef to write the book quickly, because I already have all of this content on hand.
- **Relevant:** I will be using this book to promote my restaurant as well as tourism in our area because we are focused on regional cuisine and recipes.
- **Time-bound:** I would like to publish this book by next fall so that I have it available for the holiday season.

As you can see from these two examples are two vastly different authors, using the SMART goal structure can be helpful no matter what kind of author you are. By setting out your goals in this way, you can tweak them to fit your circumstances and get a clearer picture of what it is that you want from your book project. Everyone wants to be a best seller, be a part of Oprah's book club, or get a lot of press. It's OK to have those dreams. But we all know that with millions of books being published every year those dreams aren't necessarily achievable. Start with what you know, lean into who you already are and the audience that you already have, and craft goals for your book project that are doable.

Understand Your Own Style

It's important for authors to understand their working style. Even if you haven't written a book before, you know how you like to work. And I will be the first to tell you that every single publisher and every single publishing scenario has a different culture. If you look inward and are honest with yourself about how you like to work, that can help you guide your decision on what publishing path to take. Do you like to be in control, are you a bit of a loner when it comes to work, do you have business savvy? Then self-publishing might be a perfect fit for you. Do you want a more hands-off approach where you are solely focused on writing your book? Perhaps you are a happy warrior who is ready and willing to do whatever it takes to get your book published, which includes marketing it. Maybe you want a higher royalty rate later. Do you like to surround yourself with qualified people who know more than you and can lead you through the process? Maybe traditional publishing is your jam. Or are you a blend of both? Maybe hybrid publishing is deep within your soul.

I always ask authors to do some self-work and a self-assessment to think about how we can work best together. And I think most editors do that as well. While all sizes of publishing companies have their own culture, processes, and systems that they use to produce quality work in a timely fashion, they are not so rigid that they won't be willing to work with you around your schedule and in a way that makes you feel most productive, seen, and heard.

Take some time to jot down a few notes about what it is that you want in terms of your publishing experience. Here are a few areas to consider:

- Working style
- How you like to receive feedback
- Your personal communication style
- Comfort level with constructive criticism
- Need for creative control
- Willingness to get out of your comfort zone
- Need for editorial support
- Need for marketing support
- Personal financial commitment
- Desire for extended services like foreign rights and subsidiary rights management
- Your vision for the creative and business relationship

These are just a few considerations, and your mileage may vary on each of them. Feel free to add your own style-related considerations so you can come to a clearer picture of what you want out of this process.

Consider Money Matters

An important consideration when making your decision about your publishing path is money. Each publishing path requires a different level of investment from authors, ranging from $0.00 all the way up to $100,000. Professional editing, designing, producing, printing, and distributing a book is not a cheap process. Keep in mind that it costs money to do all of these things. So, when you're trying to determine which direction you want to go in, be mindful of your budget. Are you comfortable with paying for everything? Are you comfortable with paying for the print run while a publishing partner picks up the bill for editorial and design? Maybe you don't want to pay for any of the upfront costs of producing a book at all, and would prefer to get paid on the back end of the deal. Or perhaps you don't want to pay for the editorial and production side, but you are willing to put in money for marketing or public relations. These are all things to think about as you review your options. Though your mileage may vary, and costs will change over time depending on what type of publishing partner you work with, here are some basic guidelines for what you can expect when it comes to the financial side of the equation.

SELF-PUBLISHING

If you are self-publishing, you are paying for everything. That includes:

- Editing the book
- Design of the cover and interiors
- Layout and production
- Legal fees
- Applying for an ISBN and copyright
- File and data management
- Printing
- Ebook conversion
- Audiobook production
- Distribution
- Marketing
- Public relations
- Advertising
- Reprints
- Travel

This is just a general overview of some of the expense categories that you will run into when you publish a book. This isn't to say that you have to do all of these things, but at the very least you will need to edit, design, and print your book. Pricing for all of these items can easily hit the high 5 to 6 figure mark if you're not careful. Can you do it on the cheap? Of course you can—but the end result may not be the quality product or experience for which you were hoping. Even if you work with a packager, someone is still doing these functions and still needs to get paid. So, with publishing yourself, make sure that fronting the costs for the entire process is something you're comfortable with.

HYBRID PUBLISHING

If you go with a hybrid publisher, you will share the costs of the project. The breakdown of these shared costs depends on the publisher, and the deal you make with them. Some hybrid publishers only require the author to pay for the printing of the books. Others might have the author pay for the editorial and production, or the marketing and PR side of the equation. Keep in mind that working with the hybrid publisher means you are partners in the venture so ultimately your revenue share on the back end of the project is going to be higher than if you went with the traditional publisher. That said, it's also going to be lower than if you are self-published because you are sharing the profits.

TRADITIONAL PUBLISHING

In a traditional publishing arrangement, the author pays no upfront costs. This is the kind of publishing deal that you're probably most familiar with, in which the author is paid some sort of advance and then makes royalties on the back end of the deal. This is ideal for someone who doesn't want to outlay any upfront costs, however, that means a lower royalty rate on the back end. In addition, a traditionally published author's advance has to "earn out," which means that no royalties will be paid to the author until the book has earned net revenues for the author in the amount of the advance. What this means for you is that you may have to wait quite a while before you see any royalty checks rolling in.

Check Your Ego

Let's be honest. Publishing is an ego-driven business. That isn't a bad thing, it just means that you have to be a little crazy to write a book and a little ego driven to want to do so. No one writes a book because they are feeling modest. Most people write a book because they are compelled to share their knowledge and expertise, which requires a little bit of ego.

I don't say this to suggest that you are an egomaniac. Far from the truth. You are writing a book because you are a subject-matter expert, and you have knowledge that is important to share. That said, know what the parameters of your ego are before you decide about your publishing path. If you self-publish, it can be a scrappy process. You are going to be in the weeds of the business of publishing your book. Does that jive with your ego? Will you be OK with doing that kind of legwork? If not, self-publishing may not be for you. Is your ego comfortable with being an equal partner with your publisher? If so, then hybrid publishing might be a wonderful fit for you. I've known several authors who were a little hesitant to go the hybrid route, but ended up loving it because they felt like they had a true partnership with their publisher with shared goals and shared dreams. It can be a really wonderful fit for a nonfiction author. As for traditional publishing, you don't necessarily have to have a big ego to thrive in that environment. I will advise however, that you do need to be open to constructive criticism and allowing professionals to do their jobs. When you work with the traditional publishing house, you will not get the final say on much of the editorial process nor the cover design. That can be a sticking point for some authors. Trust me when I tell you that publishing professionals know their business well. You need to be OK with trusting them to make decisions about your book that best position it for the marketplace.

A WORD ABOUT AGENTS

We've talked a lot throughout the book about different publishing paths from self-publishing and hybrid to traditional. I want to take a moment to talk about working with literary agents. Consider agents like you would brokers. They are brokers for your book, much like a real estate agent sells a house, a literary agent sells a book project. Agents work with all kinds of publishing houses from small independent presses to large international corporations. Most of them focus on a certain set of topic areas in which they have experience and confidence in selling. Working with an agent can be a positive experience because they know the publishing landscape, current trends, and have personal relationships with editors that you as an author do not. Basically, they go out and do the legwork of finding a publisher for you.

Here's how they do that. Agents have very firm, strong relationships with existing editors and publishing houses. They we'll work with you to craft a winning book proposal that best positions your book for sale to an editor. The great thing about working with an agent in addition to their street cred and deep well of contacts is that they have a lot of experience in preparing proposals. This is their livelihood after all, so they are as invested in your success as you are. When your proposal is ready, an agent will show it to relevant editors who might have interest in your book project. They then work with the editor to determine if your project is a fit for their publishing house, and if so, they will negotiate the deal on your behalf. In addition, they have extensive experience with contract language and will know what to look for when it comes to setting terms, and making sure that your intellectual property is protected. Another benefit of working with an agent is they will likely be able to get you the best terms when it comes to advance and royalties.

How do you find a reputable agent? Just as you researched publishing houses, book packagers and other publishing professionals, you should research agents. The first rule of thumb I always tell potential authors is to make sure that agents are connected to some kind of professional association and that they work on commission only. The standard commission rate for literary agents is 15% of the net receipts from your book. Never, ever work with an agent who asks you to pay them up front. If someone is asking you to do that, they are not a reputable agent, and your projects will be at risk. Literary agents are governed by the Association of Author Representatives, the AAR, which sets forth guidelines and requirements for how agents work with authors. This is an organization that looks to protect not only authors but the reputation of their member agents as well. Reputable literary agents also do not require you to work with outside parties to prepare your book for publication. Agents are free to suggest that you work with an outside editor, developmental editor, or someone who can help you prepare your proposal, but those should be no more than suggestions. If an agent requires you to work with a vendor to prepare your book for the sales process, they are not a reputable agent and are likely to get a kickback. As someone who has done her fair share of freelance editing, I have worked with many agents whose clients need some help preparing the final manuscript to turn into their editor. But in those instances, the deal is already signed, and the author needs ghostwriting help more than anything. That's a different story than having an agent require you to work with an editor before your book is even sold. There's a nuance there, so be mindful of it and be careful.

Keep in mind that a right-fit agent is going to be someone who already sells books in your category. For example, if you run across a literary agent who only sells fiction work and you are nonfiction author, that is not the agent for you because nonfiction is not their area of expertise. How do you find out what agents represent? Look on their websites, at their LinkedIn profiles, or do a quick Google search to find out what kinds of books they represent. And, just like when you were researching publishers, be a student of your competition and read acknowledgments pages and other people's books. Typically folks will thank their agents there and you can start to build a list based on books that are in your category. The AAR, the association I just mentioned, also has a list of agents that you can check out on their website.

If you were interested in working with an agent, the approach is not that different from how you would approach a publishing house. Most agents ask for a query or pitch first, and if they are interested, they will follow up with a request to see your full proposal. There are a lot of great resources out there to connect with agents, including:

- QueryTracker (querytracker.net)
- AgentQuery (agentquery.com)
- Poets & Writers Literary Agent Database (pw.org/literary_agents)
- Association of Authors' Representatives (aar.org)
- Association of American Literary Agents (aalitagents.org)

One final note: As you're considering whether or not to work with an agent, keep in mind your goals and what kind of publishing experience you are looking for. You obviously don't need an agent if you are going to self-publish and also typically not if you are going to go with a hybrid publisher. Using an agent is often reserved for those who wish to pursue a traditional publishing arrangement. Most agents I know work with both indie presses and larger houses to provide you with as many options in the traditional world as possible.

NEGOTIATE

Once you determine your publishing path, it's time to think about negotiating your deal. You'll do this no matter what you choose because everything is a business arrangement. If you are a self-publishing, you'll be talking about terms with vendors and freelancers who will help produce your book. You'll also need to negotiate with printers and distributors. When it comes to hybrid or traditional publishing, your primary source of negotiation will be with the editor who is acquiring your project. Let's unpack some of the finer points of deal negotiation now.

Field Offers

For self-publishers, you don't typically field offers from people who wish to publish your book. Why? Because you are the publisher. As such, you are the one going out to shop your project with various vendors, freelancers, or packagers. Offers look a little different here because these people are trying to get your business. Offers you may run across in the self-publishing world include:

- Editorial services
- Layout, production, and design services
- Proofreading and copy editing
- Project management
- Printing
- Shipping and logistics
- Warehousing and distribution
- Marketing and public relations
- Audiobook and translation services

Since you're operating as the publisher in this scenario, you will have to negotiate all of these various vendor contracts one-by-one as you move throughout the publication process.

If you are receiving offers from hybrid or traditional publishers, the scenario is a bit different. For hybrid publishers, the offer will typically look like a standard publishing offer but with the added layer of shared responsibilities and costs. For example, a hybrid offer may include a full offer of publication with you fronting the bill for the printing. An offer from a traditional publisher will be a bit more complex because they are taking on the financial burden of the entire project. As you receive offers from either of these types of publishers, they will typically come to you either in a deal memo first or in the form of a draft contract that you may redline with your changes. This is where the negotiation starts.

Discuss Terms

You'll begin by discussing the primary terms of the deal. Again, this doesn't necessarily apply to self-publishers because you are driving the bus here. But for hybrid and traditional publishing deals, the most common terms that will be up for negotiation include:

- Advance
- Royalties on print books
- Ebook royalties
- Audiobook royalties
- Other subsidiary rights such as magazine or anthology
- Due dates and timelines
- Editorial responsibilities of both parties
- Marketing responsibilities of both parties
- Free or discounted author copies
- Option rights on your next book
- Word count and publication date

These are just a few of the most common terms that can be negotiated in hybrid and traditional agreements.

Read the Fine Print

Publishing contracts are nothing if not complicated. In my 25-plus years in the industry I have seen all kinds of contracts. Some are fairly straightforward while others are so complicated it takes a whole team of lawyers to parse them out. Reading the fine print of what is expected of you and what your rights are in a publishing agreement is a vital skill to have. If it's a skill you yourself do not possess, then I urge you to have a lawyer assist you with the contract negotiation and redlining the contract for any items that may not benefit you. Most publishers use standard boilerplate language for issues surrounding indemnity, legal representation, representations and warranties, and procedures for pursuing legal action. You likely won't be able to redline much of this language, but you should still read it carefully to understand your rights. In particular, pay close attention to what your rights are in terms of writing other books for other publishers, your next book project, who owns the copyright, and the rights you are granting to the publisher. I've known many authors who did not read this fine print and ended up signing away their copyright to the publisher. While this doesn't prevent them from using the content in the book, it does take away their ownership of that content. Know what you are signing away before you sign on the dotted line.

WHAT TO EXPECT AFTER YOU'VE SIGNED

Typically, once contracts are signed, publishers will reach out to the author with a timeline, production schedule, and all of the relevant contact information they need as they begin to write their book. It is hard to believe that for most nonfiction authors, they have come this far and the book isn't even written yet! This is where the fun begins. In the next chapter, we'll talk a little bit about what that process looks like for each of the publishing paths.

Activity 9
YOUR PUBLISHING PATH

Use the space below to write down pros and cons of each option.

SELF-PUBLISHING

1. Goals

....
....
....
....

2. My style

....
....
....
....

3. Money matters

....
....
....
....

4. My ego

....
....
....
....

5. Negotiation considerations

....
....
....
....

HYBRID PUBLISHING

1. Goals

2. My style

3. Money matters

4. My ego

5. Negotiation considerations

TRADITIONAL PUBLISHING

1. Goals

....
....
....
....
....

2. My style

....
....
....
....
....

3. Money matters

....
....
....
....
....

4. My ego

....
....
....
....
....

5. Negotiation considerations

....
....
....
....

Launch Your Book

AFTER PUTTING IN SO MUCH WORK researching your publishing options mapping out your proposal, and writing the proposal, it's hard to believe that that is only the beginning of your journey. Once you decide which publishing path is right for you, then you are clear to move on to the next part of the process which is writing and launching your book.

Many authors are surprised to find that once a book deal is signed the process of writing and publishing it takes quite a long time. Most nonfiction books are published within 18 to 24 months of signing a contract. Some are fast-tracked and can be published sooner, especially when the material is incredibly timely like a political book that is coming out in an election year, for example. Once the writing is complete, the editorial and production process usually takes anywhere from 6 to 9 months, followed by a few months to print and get the book into distribution. The sooner you can turn in a fully fleshed out manuscript to your editor, the sooner that process can start. In this chapter, we'll talk about what happens after you sign the contract for your book project.

WRITING THE BOOK

The first order of business is writing your book. You've already done a lot of writing when you worked on your book proposal. The good news is a lot of that legwork will serve you well now that it's time to write the entire manuscript. Remember when you did the chapter summaries and wrote a sample chapter for the proposal? They are the basis for writing the full manuscript now.

The amount of time you have to write the book will depend on the publishing path you choose and the publisher with whom you work with. If you are self-publishing, the choice is really up to you regarding writing time. You could crank it out quickly and have a manuscript written in under three months or you could take your time and write the manuscript over the next year. For hybrid and traditional publishing, the publisher will dictate the writing schedule. Why is this? Publishers have a very specific timeline for each book project, and they need to work within the parameters of that timeline in order to sell the book into the retail market. So, while I can't give you and definitive answer here about how long it will take you to write the book, I can tell you that it will take anywhere from 3 to 12 months to have a fully fleshed out manuscript completed. Everyone's writing style is different, but let's cover a few useful tips that can help you along the way.

Set a Schedule

Once you know how long you have to write the book, map out a schedule for yourself. You don't want to get to the end of the writing time period and find that you don't have very much done. Earlier in the book, you read about how to determine your publishing path based on several factors including your working style. This is another time for you to consider how you work best so you can set a writing schedule for yourself that is manageable and productive.

Some people like to write early in the morning. Others are night owls. Some authors (most, in fact) have jobs outside of being a writer. If you have to work around a day job or own a small business, it will be incredibly important for you to have a firm and manageable writing schedule.

Decide how many hours each day you want to dedicate to writing your book. Some authors can write for 5 to 8 hours a day and not break a sweat. Others need to work in more manageable chunks of time, like one to two hours. You can test drive how long it takes you to write a chapter and then apply that to the word count that you need to reach for the book. Your editors should provide you with a firm final manuscript date to work towards. Use that date and work backwards to map out a schedule for yourself so that you can consistently crank out chapters.

Eat the Elephant One Bite at a Time

The idea of writing an entire book can be very overwhelming. So, once you have determined a writing schedule for yourself based on the hours that you need to work, factor in how much content you have to write. What is the easiest way for you to envision manageable success as you write? For some people it is a word count per day. For others, it may be chunks of a chapter, or whole chapters each day. Think about what makes the most sense to you and eat that elephant one bite at a time period in other words, set realistic word count or chapter goals better consistent with the amount of time you feel you can dedicate to the writing process each day.

Use Tools to Get the Job Done

Gone are the romantic days of writing out your manuscript in longhand on a legal pad. That certainly doesn't sound very romantic to me! What does sound nice, however, is finding a way to write that works best for you. There are wonderful tools available to writers these days that can help them accomplish their writing goals. One of my favorites is dictation software. In fact, I have used dictation software to write a great deal of this book. Programs like Google Docs and Microsoft Word offer a dictate function which records your words and converts them into texts. For those of us whose fingers can't keep up with our thoughts, this is an absolute game changer. It's also incredibly helpful for auditory learners who need to hear the content to make sense of it as they write.

Another great tool to use is manuscript writing software. I personally have never used them, but there are many fans out there. If you need some help structuring your chapters and creating manageable drafts of your book, such software might be useful to you.

A Word About AI

No writing tool is getting more attention, and more criticism than artificial intelligence, or AI. Tools like ChatGPT are emerging as industry disruptors for people who create content. Since publishing AI is in its infancy, we don't yet know the ramifications of using it in book production. Many publishers are starting to discourage the use of AI by including clauses in authors contracts that dictate how and when it may be used. This isn't necessarily a bad thing, because it's in everyone's best interest to have the majority of an author's work be original. That said, AI is a great tool for specific kinds of content creation like building lists or writing marketing copy for your book. We should all be mindful about its use and tread lightly until the industry can reach a consensus on how best to use it.

THE EDITORIAL PROCESS

Once you have turned in your manuscript to your publisher, the editorial process can begin in earnest. If you are self-publishing, this looks a little different because you are likely hiring the editor yourself or working with a book packager.

When you turn your manuscript in, you will be assigned a series of editors to help you through each phase of editing. Typically, there are three types of editing: developmental editing, copy editing, and proofreading. Let's unpack each one.

Developmental Editing

Developmental editing is exactly what it sounds like. It is just the development of the manuscript. In this type of editing, the focus will be on major structural and organizational aspects of your manuscript. Your editor will review the structure of the table of contents and how chapters in each section flow from one to the next. Your editor will also consider the order and arrangement of chapters. Some books are dependent on a strict structure, especially more prescriptive or how-to books. Others are a bit more freewheeling, and there is not as much pressure to put topics in a certain order. A developmental editor will also work on paragraph-level transitions as well as overall tone, voice, tense, and the general effect of the reading experience. Consider this the 30,000-foot-view edit where the focus is on the big picture items.

Copyediting

Copy editing narrows the editorial funnel to focus on sentence level and paragraph level issues. The copy editor will assess general readability and conduct a robust line edit with a focus on syntax, grammar, spelling, and transitions. Some copy editors will even conduct simple fact checking as well as confirming names, common dates, and titles mentioned in the book. If your book includes end notes, footnotes, or bibliography, the copy editor will also ensure that those references are in the correct format whether that is MLA, APA, or Chicago Style. The copy editor will also be tracking queries using the comment feature either Microsoft Word or Google Docs. This allows the conversation to happen right on the page so that you can coordinate with the copy editor on any questions they may have.

Proofreading

Once you get to the proofreading stage, the focus is on dotting i's and crossing t's. You are not working on organizational issues where you are moving around large blocks of texts at this point. The proofreader should be laser focused on finding any last-minute typos, misspellings, or other issues that may impact the understanding and readability of the text. This is not the time to decide you don't like a chapter and then replace it with a new chapter. This is the time where you must get granular and focus on the most important last-minute issues.

THE PRODUCTION PROCESS

After the editorial process, your book will move into production. This is a fancy way of saying that your publisher or packager is going to design the interior pages and the cover of the book. Many authors consider the production process to be somewhat mysterious, but it's actually really straightforward. I like to tell authors this is the part of the process where your book actually starts to look like a real book. It's an extremely exciting time because something that has been a nebulous idea for so long is finally coming to life. Authors are typically not very involved in the production process—at least not as much as they are in the editorial process. Keep in mind that if you are working with a hybrid or traditional publisher, you likely won't have the final say in what your book actually looks like. Take heart because there is a reason for that. It is a publisher's job to create a product that can sell at online retailers and on the shelves. A lot of thought and research goes into how each and every book looks both on the inside and on the outside to maximize its sales potential. Trust your publisher during this process. They have your books' best interests at heart.

Cover Design

This is one of the most exciting parts of the book production process. I admit it is one of my favorites for sure! I love seeing how a designer takes the vision for a book and creates something highly visual from that concept. If you are self-publishing your book, you will have 100% creative control over this process. But again, I urge you to defer to people who have done this for many years and who have a deep well of experience and book cover design. There are so many small unspoken details that go into a book cover to help it catch the eye of readers in a bookstore or online. While you may have personal preferences that you like or things that you dislike, those aren't necessarily data points for how a book cover should be designed. Your publisher, if you are working with hybrid or traditional, will include you in the process to some degree. Often, they will ask if you have any inspiration to share with the cover designer, a color scheme that may be important to your branding, for any no-go items that you don't want to include on the cover. Beyond that, the choices will be up to them, and you will be presented with either a final cover that you don't have a say in, or with two to three options that you can have some input on before the final decision is made.

Interior Design

The interior of your book will be designed to complement the look and feel of the cover. This usually involves using similar or the same fonts as what you see on the cover for the sake of consistency. Most designers I work with like to take a sample chapter from the book to create a cover design for final approval before laying out the entire book. The manuscript that you have already turned in should denote any special elements that you want to include in the interior design of your book, like sidebars, pull quotes, or call out boxes. Your manuscript should also identify any places where a photograph or an illustration is going to go so the designer can work those elements into this interior design before presenting it to you for approval. Once everybody is on board with the final cover and the final interior look and feel, your designer can move into actually laying out the book.

Layout

There really isn't much for you as an author to do during the layout phase except wait. This is when your designer will be working hard to flow text into the existing design, size and add photos and illustrations, and make sure that the presentation of the book is what the publisher (or you, if you are self-publishing) wants. The designer may circle back to you from time to time to clarify any questions they may have about your intended placement of different items within the manuscript.

Final Proofreading

Final proofreading happens when the book is completely laid out into pages and looks the way it will once it is printed. This is your absolute final opportunity to make any last-minute changes. Your focus should be solely on must-fix issues like typos, spelling mistakes, or any critical design flaws. Most designers will send you a PDF that you can then mark up with comments, additions, or deletions. If you are not savvy about marking up a PDF, there are several YouTube videos available that can walk you through what to do.

GETTING READY FOR DISTRIBUTION

Get excited because it is almost time to hand the book off to the printer. Things really start to get real when you realize that you're going to have to make plans to print and distribute your book. If you are self-publishing, remember that this, like everything else along the way, is entirely up to you. If you plan to sell your book at traditional retailers online, working with a distributor is key to your success. That means you will have to research various distributors and choose one with which to work. Or, if you just want to have your book available to sell at back of room events, on your website, or your friends and family, the distribution piece isn't as important to you. For those working with hybrid and traditional publishers, the distribution piece will likely be handled by the publisher and not you. That said, it's good practice to at least know what that process looks like.

Printing

There's a process for selecting a printer. If you are self-publishing, you will be the person in charge of reviewing quotes and making a final choice on a printer. Most printers will quote print runs ranging from 2,500 copies all the way up to 20,000 or more copies. The more copies you buy, the lower the price per book cost is, providing you with a better deal in the long run. If you are doing a shorter print run, under 2,500 copies, your price per book will be more.

A few things have to happen before a printer can take your book project and print it. Your designer we'll need to make sure that all of the pages are in the correct order and that their files meet the requirements of the printer. The majority of books are designed using Adobe InDesign, so your designer will want to coordinate with the printer to ensure that their InDesign files are in the format and size acceptable to the printer.

Once the final design files are ready to go, your designer will probably upload them to a shared Dropbox or FTP site housed by the printer. These files tend to be incredibly large and are not appropriate to send via e-mail. Before you choose a printer, make sure you've done your due diligence and looked into each of your choices first. The printer you choose should have experience printing the style of book on which you are working. For example, if a printer cannot produce a high-quality hardback and that is what you want, then they are not the right printer for you.

When selecting a printer for your project, make sure you understand not only their pricing but their timeline as well. If you do plan to distribute your book widely, your warehouse of choice may have requirements about when the books can be accepted into the warehouse and how long it will take for them to show as being on sale at online retailers.

Distribution

Distribution is a vital element of your publishing experience. Distribution is how your book gets added to the marketplace so customers can see them on the bookshelves in their bookstore or an online retailer websites. Distributors not only house your books in their warehouse, they also pick, pack, and ship your books to retailers around the world.

The type of distribution you use for your book project will depend largely on your goals and what kind of publisher you are working with. If you are self-publishing, you will likely work with a smaller, independent distributor who can handle special orders and keep your costs low. If you are working with a hybrid or traditional publisher, they most likely are connected to a larger distribution network that has extensive contacts and partnerships throughout the world to ship and sell books. Each distributor has one or more warehouses where they house your books until they are sold. Some distributors have one massive warehouse, while others have several dotting the globe. If your goal is to sell your book internationally, a larger distributor with this kind of network will be useful to you.

Once your books are printed, they are shipped to your distributor's warehouse so orders can be fulfilled. Orders typically come in on a rolling basis, and books are picked, packed, and shipped in the order those requests are received. Your distributor will also manage sales of your ebook and possibly your audiobook as well.

Metadata

The book industry runs on metadata. If you aren't familiar with what metadata is, here's a quick overview. As soon as your book is signed, the publisher will begin to gather vital information about the book project, including:

- Specs for the book including price, trim size, and page count
- Title and subtitle
- Descriptive information

- Author biography
- Key selling points
- Marketing information
- Public relations information
- Descriptions of related content areas, known as BISAC codes
- On-sale date
- Information on author events and opportunities for special sales

All of this information is entered into the publishers or distributors database of book information. That information is then fed out to any retailers who have signed up to receive that data. Every time you see a product listing on an online retailer site, know that it is coming to that retailer via book metadata. Your publisher will be the source of truth for all of this information (or you will be if you are self-publishing) so anytime that information needs to be updated it will come from the publisher first. Most publishers work in tandem with their distributor to ensure the accuracy of the metadata. This metadata is also used by distributors to share vital specs and release information with retailers. For example, if the publication date of your book changes, it will have to be noted in the metadata so retailers can get that information quickly and accurately. Metadata isn't something you necessarily need to know a lot about if you are working with a hybrid or traditional publisher. The professionals will take care of this part for you, but it is useful to know what it is and why it's important. If you choose to self-publish, you will be responsible for your own metadata. If you plan to distribute your book widely, there are several services that can help you ensure that your metadata is entered correctly and fed to whatever distributor you plan to use.

PREPARING FOR LAUNCH

The book is written. The printed books have been shipped from the printer to the warehouse. Your distributor is preparing orders to send out to retailers. Now comes the fun part—getting ready to launch your book!

Preparations for your book launch should start at least three to six months before the publication date. Why? It's really important to lay the proper groundwork for publicity and marketing well in advance of your publication date so your book gets the attention it deserves. I'm not going to go into great detail about marketing in general here (that's a whole other book!), But I do want to walk you through some basics for how you can set your book up for a successful launch.

The rule of thumb I always share with authors is that as soon as your book is off to the printer, that is the time to switch your brain to marketing mode. Of course, having a marketing mindset from day one is important. Remember when you wrote the marketing section of your book proposal? Now is the time to refer back to that so that you can map out that plan in real time. The key to a successful book launch is to build excitement in advance of the publication date. Below are my top three recommendations for how you can create a successful book launch.

Shore Up Socials and Website

Step one is to make sure all of your socials and your website are in good working order. We talked earlier about the importance of having a landing page and a website for your book as well as using social media to promote it. If you have a personal presence on social media, I encourage you to also add a professional presence. Most platforms will let you have more than one profile and you can set one up to be purely professional to not only promote your book to promote your author brand as well. You can start to build excitement for your book a few months before publication by sharing some fun posts about your publishing journey.

As far as your website is concerned, simple is best. If you don't already have a professional website setup, you can make one easily with a program like Wix or Squarespace. Your professional website should have the following elements to best promote your book:

- Clear image of your book cover
- Brief description of the book content
- Author bio page
- Links to all of your social media
- Links to purchase your book at major retailers
- Brief sample or excerpt from your book

- Table of contents
- Relevant testimonials or blurbs from notable people within your content area
- Early reviews of your book
- A place where site visitors to sign up for more information or your newsletter if you have one

This website will be the home base for your book and everything about it. Remember to update it often, especially if you are participating in events or book signings.

Create a Content Calendar

In advance of the book launch, I highly recommend setting up a content calendar. A content calendar is simply a calendar that is focused on information that you are going to share on your social media and your website. It's a great way to structure pre-launch posts that will help drive traffic to the bookstores and to your book's website.

You don't have to be a social media guru to create and execute a successful content calendar. It could be as simple as posting something once a week on your social media handles. Or, if you want to get more involved, you can have a different kind of post every day leading up to the book launch. The goal here is to entice people to want to know more about your book—not overwhelm them with content that is not meaningful to them. Determine the cadence that best fits your goals and your abilities and run with it.

What works well for many authors is a three-month content calendar leading up to publication date with the following breakdowns of content:

- **Three months out:** Teaser posts about your work in progress, glimpses into your writing and publishing process, cover reveal, and early testimonials.
- **Two months out:** Early testimonials and kudos, recommendations for books you love, links to pre-order the book, updates on events and pre-launch giveaways.
- **Month leading up to pub date:** Presale campaign links, special

incentives to pre-order, unboxing video of your book, and a final countdown in the days leading up to pub date.

Set Up a Presale Campaign

In the content calendar section, you may have noticed that I mentioned the word presale. A presale campaign is vital to the success of your book's launch, especially if you are hoping to get online retailers to give more attention to your book and their algorithms. Getting people to order your book in advance of its publication date is a great way to build excitement and to bump up the visibility and searchability of your book online.

As soon as your metadata is feeding our online retailers, people will be able to pre-order your book. Send friends, family, and social media followers to online retailers so they can pre-order the book. There is typically an incentive for people to pre-order the book, because there will be a deep discount applied if they do so. I always tell authors to be retailer agnostic during this process. What does that mean? It means that you should send your followers to multiple retailers so your book gets widespread attention.

There are all kinds of ways you can incentivize people to pre-order your book in advance. You can do a fun and simple giveaway of something like a digital download or digital bonus chapter of your book. You can do a raffle or sweepstakes for people who have pre-ordered. The possibilities are endless.

Another part of your presale campaign should be requesting online book reviews from your readers. The more positive reviews you have with online retailers, the more visibility your book gets. As you are asking people to preorder your book, also make the ask for them to write a review for you. This is a simple, and free way for you to get great coverage with online retailers and to provide you with glowing testimonials that will help sell your book.

LAUNCH DAY!

This is it. This is the day you have been working toward and waiting for. Launch day is here! You have completed all 10 steps of the pitch to print process, and your book is out in the world. Congratulations!

Launch day is the culmination of all of your hard work. It may seem impossible that this day is finally here, but it is. Most authors find that launch day is actually a fairly quiet day in the life of their book. All of the work leading up to this point is done. The marketing has been in place for months. You have unboxed the book, had a successful presale campaign, and are now ready to claim the title of published author. My advice to authors for launch day is to simply enjoy the moment. It is the one day in the life of your book where you can sit back, relax and be grateful for the journey you have been on, and prepare for the journey ahead. Soak it up, enjoy every moment, and yes—rest. Because tomorrow, the next phase of your publishing journey begins—marketing your book for the long term. And as I mentioned before that's a whole other book. Looks like I better get to work on my next proposal!

ACKNOWLEDGMENTS

A BOOK is a team effort and wow—do I have an amazing team. Thank you to my partner in Broad Book Group, Vanessa Campos, for the constant support and dedication to our little publishing company that could. I love working with you each and every day. To Emily Carpenter-Pulskamp, my friend of more than 30 years and our fantastically talented PR guru, thank you for being my OG publishing partner in crime. We have come a long way since those late production nights in the Woods room in Le Fer Hall. I love the women we have become! To Andrew Welyczko for always joining this crazy pirate ship when we need him and producing absolutely beautiful work every damn time. To Vicky Vaughn Shea for her gorgeous design sensibility and enthusiasm for BBG. To Jim Eber for always supporting us and being a total mensch always. Thank you to Angela Maclean, our phenomenal client relations manager at Publishers Group West, for believing in BBG from day one and supporting us with unbounded enthusiasm. Thank you to the whole PGW team for your support and partnership.

I have been fortunate to work with so many talented, dedicated publishing professionals over the years. There are so many amazing editors, agents, and distribution/sales folks from whom I have been privileged to learn. Most of all, thank you to the woman who gave me my first job in publishing, Nancy Niblack Baxter. She taught me the business from the ground up and instilled a love of publishing in me that I tap into each and every day.

Thank you to my wonderful village of strong, fierce women. Ann, Rachael, and Kelly: I love being lifelong band mom besties with you. Laura and Ange: Thank you for being the sisters I never had. Meghan: You shine so brightly. Thank you for being a light in my life from the moment we met. And to my lifelong BFF, Holly: Thank you for being the most amazing sister, support system, travel buddy, and auntie. I love you beyond words, my dear.

I am beyond lucky to have a stellar bunch of humans to call my family. Mike: God love you, good man. Thank you for the never-ending patience, support, and love you give me on this crazy journey. I love you endlessly. To Will, Cate, and Vivian: Thank you for putting up with Mom's late nights, Zoom calls, and book hoarding. I always dreamed of you, and here you are—wonderful beyond my wildest dreams. And to Mom: My love for you simply cannot be put into words. There would be no us without you. Our family is a story, and you are the author. Thank you for writing it.

ABOUT THE AUTHOR

DR. JENNIFER DORSEY has worked in book publishing for over 25 years. Specializing in nonfiction, she has worked for both small presses and large national publishers in the history, tech, lifestyle, self-help, business, and professional development categories. In addition to working in the business side of publishing, she has also co-authored, revised, and ghostwritten books in the medical, business, and personal growth categories. She is a graduate of Saint Mary-of-the-Woods College and earned her M.A. and Ph.D. in rhetoric and composition at Saint Louis University. She lives in Illinois with her husband, three children, and English bulldog, Mabel. Visit **www.drjendorsey.com** to learn more.

RESOURCES

THE PUBLISHING COMMUNITY is chock-full of amazing, useful resources for writers. From magazines and blogs to editors and courses, you can absolutely find someone to lend you an assist on your publishing journey. While there is a lot of competition out there, I believe in an abundance mindset with a shared goal of educating writers about the industry we all love. That said, please keep in mind that you should always be cautious, and fully vet anyone with whom you wish to work.

With that in mind, I'm sharing some of my favorite resources below.

BOOKS
- *Bird by Bird* by Anne Lamott
- *Dreyer's English: An Utterly Correct Guide to Clarity and Style* by Benjamin Dreyer
- *Everything's An Argument* by Andrea Lunsford and John J. Ruszkiewicz
- *Jeff Herman's Guide to Book Publishers, Editors, & Literary Agents* by Jeff Herman
- *On Writing* by Stephen King
- *The Business of Being a Writer* by Jane Friedman

PERIODICALS
Creative Nonfiction: creativenonfiction.org
Library Journal: libraryjournal.com
Poets & Writers: pw.org
Publishers Weekly: publishersweekly.com
Writer's Digest: writersdigest.com

ASSOCIATIONS

- Alliance of Independent Authors: allianceindependentauthors.org
- American Booksellers Organization: bookweb.org
- American Society of Journalists and Authors: asja.org
- Association of American Literary Agents: aalitagents.org
- Association of American Publishers: publishers.org
- Association of American University Presses: aaupnet.org
- Association for Women in Communications: womcom.org
- Authors Guild: authorsguild.org
- Independent Book Publishers Association: ibpa-online.org
- International Publishers Association: internationalpublishers.org
- International Women's Writing Guild: iwwg.com
- Nonfiction Authors Association: nonfictionauthorsassociation.com
- National Speakers Association: NSAspeaker.org
- National Writers Union: nwu.org
- Society for Scholarly Publishing: sspnet.org

SAMPLE BOOK PROPOSAL

BELOW IS A sample book proposal that I put together based on one of my own areas of subject-matter expertise, feminist rhetoric. As a "recovering academic," I am tapping into my research in women's forms of communication here, and my author platform includes that part of my professional world. This example is structured in a way that breaks down the author platform into a couple of different sections since the subject matter is heavily focused on academic research and presentation.

Sister Resisters: The Badass Women of History Who Took on Religion, Misogyny, and Politics

By Jennifer Dorsey, Ph.D.

OVERVIEW

Resistance is everywhere these days. You can see it—in the images of people taking to the streets. You can hear it—in the voices of youth, leading a new generation of activists. You can feel it—in the air, electrified with the sounds of chanting, the drumbeat of a new era of civil disobedience.

It feels new. It feels necessary. It feels now.

Resistance work is, at heart, a fight against the System (with a capital S). It is the underdog fighting the Establishment. It is a group of bold women linking arms and starting their first day on the job in Washington. It is Gandhi in a prison cell refusing to eat. It is a rag-tag group of French guerilla fighters in WWII blowing up a Nazi supply line. It is... a religious cause.

It's true.

Resistance has deeper roots than we ever imagined. From the time one man or group has attempted to impose their way of life, their beliefs or their morals on any other group, there have been resisters. This book, **Sister Resisters**, will focus keenly on women. Specifically, the strong, sometimes subversive women who resisted the eons of misogyny, suppression, and oppression metered out by the world's great religions.

From saints and nuns to rabbis and laypersons, history shows us that women have a long tradition of resisting systems from the inside out.

Sister Resisters: The Badass Women of History Who Took on Religion, Misogyny and Politics thrills and inspires readers by bringing to life the women who were brave enough to stand up for what they believed was right. Told in short mini bios that illuminate the lives, the courage, and the social systems they were fighting against, this compelling book will flip the history told by the victors (the men) on its head. Turns out, *all religious women are not pious, quiet, and submissive*. There are thousands of "Sister Resisters" hidden in history. Some are legendary, some still castigated. Some our modern era holds up as heroines. There are thousands of these women whose stories have been muffled or muddied, forgotten but never forgiven. Women who were bold, courageous, and "stubborn." They were abused, shunned, defrocked, disemboweled, crucified, burned at the stake and their memories were ground under the heels of the Establishment. These victorious vixens were castigated for their initiative and mocked for their willingness to stand up for what they believed was right.

Sister Resisters are doing it by themselves. And they've been doing it for centuries. Look under that hassock, you'll find a tough-as-nails woman with a plan. Don't be fooled by the rosary, the mala beads, or the hymnal in her hands. This girl's got power and she's going to use it.

This book will highlight female disruptors from various faith traditions throughout history. From ancient Aspasia and medieval Julian of Norwich to contemporary religious figures like the women from Nuns on the Bus, *Sister Resisters* will let readers cavort through their compelling tales of courage. They'll meet some badass religious women who shouted their truth through action, many of whom have not yet been directly linked to the idea of resistance or activism, women who have been claimed for religion but not yet for resistance.

Readers will meet women like Ray Frank, Girl Rabbi of the Golden West, who was one of the first women to preach publicly and open doors for women to serve as rabbis in the Jewish faith.

Readers will find out about current Sister Resisters like members of the Nuns on the Bus coalition who give new meaning to the term "holy rollers" with their brave, public bus tour focused on progressive protest and civil disobedience, both religious and political.

Other Sister Resisters featured in the book include: Mary Baker Eddy, Sor Juana Ines de la Cruz, Tekawitha, Dorothy Day, the Bhumata Brigade, and Catherine of Siena.

While all these women come from different faith traditions, they all share a fighting spirit, thirst for social justice, and fearless ingenuity that have been the hallmarks of resistance throughout history. Perhaps, these true stories will even inspire readers to speak out against the injustice they see around them in our modern era.

A fun, fresh, irreverent look at these badass religious women is long overdue. Readers who enjoy their historical how-to content with a dash of irreverence and a well-placed swear word here and there will be a primary audience for this book. The success of books like Jen Sincero's *You Are A Badass* (selling over 648,000 in 2017) proves that boldness still wins and people still yearn to be inspired to be their authentic selves.

By stripping off the veneer of religiosity and our erroneous but common misperceptions of what it means to be a woman in a religious life, readers will see these amazing women for what they were—first-generation disruptors who knew the risks but took them anyway. We stand on the shoulders of Giantesses. Everyone has the right to know about them.

MARKET ANALYSIS

Sister Resisters has a wide market reach not only for those interested in social and political activism, but also for the segment of people who are stuck in some type of system (from corporate to religious to educational) and want to resist the status quo. It will appeal to women who are conscious of feeling entrapped in a system that does not honor or respect them. It could become required reading for Women's Studies courses, in secular and parochial schools and universities.

Sister Resisters will raise a rallying flag in the hearts of all who deeply desire change. According to a 2017 NPR report, political activism in the U.S. has been on a sharp ascent since the 2016 election. Progressive activism in particular has risen at a rate never seen before in American politics, according to Dana Fisher, a University of Maryland sociologist interviewed for the piece who has studied large-scale protests. In January of 2017, over 500,000 women participated in the Women's March in Washington D.C. alone (with millions more participating worldwide). Fisher interviewed 500 of them and, shockingly, more than 30 percent said that they had never protested anything before in their lives. Such an uptick is a clear indicator of the current climate of activism.

This exploration of how historical religious women resisted appeals to audiences interested in the history, religion, and women's interest categories. According to *Publishers Weekly*, the history category grew by a healthy 13 percent in 2017, with books related to the popularity of *Hidden Figures* helping make that happen (women for the win, again). Also of note is the fact that women's studies topics are no longer merely academic in tone but have reached the mainstream. Compendium-style books about high-achieving women, such as the wildly popular *Women in Science* (selling over 128,000 units in 2017) and *Rad American Women A-Z* continue to show that books featuring badass women are here to stay. What's missing in the competitive mix is a book that joins these stories of influential activists (religious ones, especially) with a strong action plan for the reader.

TABLE OF CONTENTS

- Chapter 1: Overview
- Chapter 2: Recognize Your Place and Power
- Chapter 3: Aspasia on Flipping the Silence Script
- Chapter 4: Dorothy Day on Doing the Small Work
- Chapter 5: Saint Kateri Tekawitha on Laying the Groundwork
- Chapter 6: Sor Juana Ines de la Cruz on Unnerving with Cleverness and Humor
- Chapter 7: Ray Frank, Girl Rabbi, on Building Your Ethos Brand
- Chapter 8: Trupthi Desai on Getting in Good Trouble

CHAPTER SUMMARIES

Chapter 1: Overview

The first chapter sets a basis for the book by introducing the reader to what it means to be a "Sister Resister" and connecting our modern notion of resistance to the long thread of historical religious and political resistance. The reader will be introduced to the women they'll meet in the book. They will see the "systems with a capital S" that these women fought, usually from within: what they are/were, where and how they operate, and how to understand women's place in them. To connect with the reader and set up the promise of the book, I tell the story of how I first got to know some of these women through my own research and personal resistance journey and how I found a way to model a resistance framework based on those lives. I intend to ignite reader's need for forging a resistance action plan of their own and join with her to show heroic examples of women who have come before us.

Chapter 2: Recognize Your Place and Power

This chapter is all about placing the reader into the narrative thread and tradition of Sister Resisters. Here, the goal is to encourage the reader to recognize where she is part of the systems—religious, professional, socioeconomic, or political—and help her examine whether she needs to resist it/change it/modify it to encompass everyone, especially women. In the #MeToo era, women need to know that we are not collectively nor individually powerless in the face of the entrenched systems that provide life support to our world. Chapter 2 includes a self-assessment that will help the reader identify and come to terms with her place in the system and identify what her resistance "style" could be based on the women who will be highlighted in the book. We each have a place in the system, whether it holds us back or allows us to benefit. Before we can change it, we must know where we stand, if the system needs changing and where, and then find a "badass" woman who models that type of resistance and map out a plan for how to use our strength for good not just for us, but for others. Chapter 2 will show the reader that Sister Resisters is an inspiring, motivating call to action she can use to examine and reform the world in which she lives.

At the end of this chapter, I exhort women to consider their power to effect change as individuals through the examples of those who have gone before us, and to reconnect her to her own strength to revitalize, reconstruct and if necessary, revolt against unfair systems.

Chapter 3: Aspasia on Flipping the Silence Script

Silence is powerful. While we tend to think of it as a bad thing (to be frank, silencing others is never a pro-badass move), silence can sometimes be used to achieve resistance goals. This chapter addresses how to flip the script on silence, as well as how to uncover voices of those who have been unwillingly silenced and bring their resistance moves into the light. In this chapter, the reader meets Aspasia (470 BC–400 BC), stateswoman of Athens and wife of Pericles. Aspasia, though an influential rhetorician and thinker, was silenced in Athenian culture just because she was a woman. Today, she is believed to have been influential in the later works of Socrates, Plato, and Aristophanes among others, though she was never given proper credit for her influence. Scholars now believe that she not only influenced, but quite possibly wrote, many of the common tenets of Greek philosophy we know today. She flew under the radar, and by doing so, impacted Western thinking as we know it today. The phrase "for most of history, Anonymous was a woman" sums up Aspasia and why her influence is there and always has been.

Chapter 4: Dorothy Day on Doing the Small Work

Anyone who does resistance work will tell you that not every day is full of marches and social media-worthy action posts. Most days are focused on doing the everyday mundane tasks associated with resisting a system. This chapter shows the reader how to do that, no matter what system she is trying to change. No Sister Resister models this better than Dorothy Day (1897–1980), Catholic social activist, key figure of the Catholic Worker Movement, and founder of the *Catholic Worker* newspaper. Day performed the small, everyday actions that build up to resistance on a global scale, most notably helping move the American Catholic Church into the modern social justice movement by focusing on economic injustice and putting faith into action not only for Catholics, but people of all faiths. For Day, every movement, every action was in service to her political activism (which, ironically, focused on a pacifist viewpoint) as modeled through her Catholic faith. In Chapter 4, the reader will get to know Day and her model for making resistance a part of daily life.

Chapter 5: Saint Kateri Tekawitha on Laying the Groundwork

Coalition building is a key to resisting from the inside. The reader can't go it alone—she needs a squad. This chapter focuses on how to build your resistance crew, whether you're fighting for better pay at work or putting together a "letter to the editor" club for the next election cycle. To provide a model for coalition building, the reader will meet Saint Kateri Tekawitha (1656–1680), an Algonquin-Mohawk laywoman who converted to Catholicism at 19 and moved to the Jesuit mission village of Khanawake near what is now Montreal. Though her native background seemed an unusual match for a Catholic life, Tekawitha worked to build broad coalitions with the Jesuits and non-native populations of Canada. In particular, she formed an alliance with a fellow missionary, Marie-Therese, with whom she partnered to minister to native associates and spread the Catholic faith. Though told by the Jesuits that they were not yet mature enough in their faith to take on the work, they did it anyway, in total badass style.

Chapter 6: Sor Juana Ines de la Cruz on Unnerving with Cleverness and Humor

Oppressors hate humor. They do **not** have the humor gene—unless *they* are making the jokes. Nor do they appreciate Hermione Granger-like cleverness. So, you know what that means? You can totally use it to disarm them. This chapter is all about channeling your inner Hermione to knock architects of the System off balance for good. Or, better yet, channeling your inner Sor Juana, who used her wit and writing prowess to call out and disarm the bishop of Puebla, who had not only published her writing without her permission but also criticized it publicly using a pseudonym to protect his own identity. Mimicking his approach, Sor

Juana penned *Reply to Sor Philotea* in what was at the time a stunning rebuke of patriarchal and clerical power. In it, she denounced his views and defended women's rights to education. Using humor and an ironic and uncanny parody of the bishop's letter, Sor Juana gives us a roadmap for channeling our inner smartass to disarm our oppressors.

Chapter 7: Ray Frank, Girl Rabbi, on Building Your Ethos Brand

If you've ever taken a first-year comp course, you learn all about ethos. Yes, it refers to ethics but, more importantly, it speaks to authority. Who has authority? You do, Sister Resister! You can be the expert on any topic within the System—all you must do is show them your street cred. If you want to resist, this chapter shows you how to harness the power of your own knowledge base and get your RESPECT by building your personal ethos brand. Though you may not have heard of Ray Frank, Girl Rabbi of the Golden West (1861–1948), you can learn a thing or two from her when it comes to personal brand building. Frank built her brand in the California Jewish community, where she taught Bible studies and Jewish history to notables like Gertrude Stein. But it was her first public speaking engagement in Spokane, Washington in 1890, where she earned her street cred as the first woman to publicly preach from a pulpit. Though never interested in formal ordination, she continued to speak and preach throughout the country until her death in 1948, and deeply influenced the movement to ordain women. Generations of women rabbis stand on her shoulders. She demanded respect as an equal in the pulpit and earned it for those who followed.

Chapter 8: Trupthi Desai on Getting in Good Trouble

As civil rights pioneer John Lewis likes to say, sometimes you must get in "good trouble." You've got to shake things up a bit to get the system to right itself (or at least give a little). From sit-ins and marches to saying your piece at the next city council meeting, this chapter talks all about how to get over your damn self and put your body on the line for a cause. That's what Trupthi Desai (1985–) and her Bhumata Brigade do today. Founded in 2010 by Desai, an Indian gender equality activist, this activist organization in state of Maharashtra, India is dedicated to fighting against injustice to women and corruption. They are most well known for their protests against the banning of women from worshipping at places of worship. Every day, members of the 4,000-woman-coalition put their bodies on the line to bring attention to matters of injustice and are subject to physical violence, arrest, and censure. If they can do it, you can do it.

Chapter 9: Sister Simone Campbell on Using the Master's Tools

Original Sister Resister Audrey Lorde wrote about how to dismantle the master's house using the master's tools. In other words, how can we use what the System has put in place to take it apart for good? This chapter of the book brings many of the lessons from previous chapters together to show how you can take what the systematic architects have built and use them to your own advantage. The best exemplars of bringing all of these tools together are the women from Nuns on the Bus, a group of Catholic nuns lead by Sister Simone Campbell (1945–) who tour the country on a bus (literally, nuns on a bus) to bring attention to the systems that seek to oppress those impacted by social justice issues of economic inequality, healthcare, immigration, and voter suppression among others. By using the tools provided by the system of the Catholic Church (money, exposure, publicity, etc.), Sister Simone and her Nuns on the Bus have been able to slowly chip away at and bring attention to the systematic disenfranchisement of the most vulnerable among us—especially women. The Vatican under Benedict XVI's leadership once called out Nuns on the Bus for having "serious doctrinal problems" and "radical feminist themes incompatible with the Catholic faith." Sounds like a ringing endorsement for the penultimate chapter of Sister Resisters to me!

Chapter 10: Your Sister Resister Action Plan

Now, go **do** the thing! This chapter lays out the action items and steps you need, taking cues from our badass women in religion, to create your own plan of resistance. The chapter will include a baseline plan that you can adapt for any System, along with some example plans for common systematic hot spots in the workplace, place of worship, school, and local/state government. Every plan will include a fancy-ass infographic that can be shared widely on social.

COMPETITIVE ANALYSIS
Nasty Women: Feminism, Resistance, and Revolution in Trump's America
Edited by Samhita Mukhopadhyay and Kate Harding (Picador, 2017)
ISBN 978-1250155504
Amazon Sales Ranking: 28,311

This is an excellent compendium of essays from notable feminist writers that digs into the "why" behind how women got to the place in history where 53 percent of white women voted for Trump and 94 percent of black women voted for Hillary Rodham Clinton. Essays from Cheryl Strayed, Rebecca Solnit, and a variety of intersectional women writers address the deep divides among women, the current state of women's resistance, and what we can do to move forward as women in a changed world. The variety of voices speaks to the need for an intersectional approach to fighting against the systematic oppression of all women—not just white ones.

However, *Nasty Women* suffers from a lack of focus and direction, which is not surprising considering its structure as a collection of essays. While the individual essays offer analysis and hope, the book does not provide the reader with a tangible, action-oriented narrative. The essays are compelling but leave the reader wondering how to apply the lessons to their own resistance plan.

Sister Resisters does provide that application, leading readers through the narrative arcs of women resisters while showing them how those lessons directly apply to their own efforts of resistance. By tying each woman's story to an actionable task of resistance work, the book allows readers to see themselves doing the work, not just reading about how others have resisted.

Rad Women Worldwide
Kate Schatz (Ten Speed Press, 2016)
ISBN 978-0399578861
Amazon Sales Ranking: 14,299

This compendium of badass women from all over the world is an enjoyable read with attractive illustrations. As appropriate for middle-grade readers as grown women, it does a solid job of introducing the reader to women from various cultures who have made resistance their calling card. From the *New York Times* bestselling author of *Rad American Women A-Z*, this book shows readers that feminist resistance is not new, nor a uniquely American idea by featuring 40 women who made strides in the intersectional feminist movement, from 16th-century sea captain Granuaile O'Malley to Nazi-fighter Sophie Scholl.

However, the book has its limitations, most notably in scope and depth. Featuring 40 women in a book that is designed to appeal to multiple ages means that there is little room for analysis of these women and their work. Rather, it serves as a conversation starter, a survey course, of intersectional resistance work. In this way, it achieves the goal of introducing the reader to these women but falls short in drawing the reader into each story and allowing the reader to connect personally to the subject.

Sister Resisters will not only provide an introduction to women resisters but explore their resistance work in the broader context of historical narrative and efficacy of that work for modern applications. Since each woman is tied to a particular aspect of how to resist a system, the analysis of each will include that context so readers can not only draw a connection to them personally, but to how the systems they fought against are still prevalent today.

The Little Book of Feminist Saints
Julia Pierpont (Random House, 2018)
ISBN 978-0399592744
Amazon Sales Ranking: 63,507
This is a charming collection of short biographies with illustrations of secular feminist "saints." At first glance, one might think this is just another book of saints, but no. This book turns the idea of "saint" on its head and bestows the title on secular feminists ranging from Audre Lorde to Billie Jean King. Pocket-sized with beautiful illustrations, this book is a lovely re-imagining of the concept of what a saint can (and should) be.

However, as is the case with other books in this style, the content only scratches the surface of who these women are. In addition, the short biographies leave the reader wondering how to connect these women to the broader context of the modern feminist story. More inspirational than aspirational, this book falls short of its goal to remake these notable women into feminist saints by not drawing a clear connection between their actions and attributes.

Sister Resisters makes that connection clear and charts a course from ancient religious life to modern-day resistance work. By highlighting both the biographies and historical backgrounds of the systems they fought against, readers are taken on a rich journey of religious resistance work over time. In addition, each woman featured will be directly tied to an action women can take in their own lives to buck these systems from the inside out. These stories are not only narrative in nature—they are roadmaps for doing the work of resistance.

You are a Badass: How to Stop Doubting Your Greatness and Start Living an Awesome Life
Jen Sincero (Running Press, 2013)
ISBN 978-0762447695
Amazon Sales Ranking: 98

You are a Badass helps readers nurture their authentic selves and recognize their inner badass. More importantly, though, it allows readers to acknowledge the stasis of the lives they live and create a path forward that gives them permission to honor parts of their interior lives that they've always been told are bad, wrong, or inappropriate. It's a manifesto on resisting the idea of the "proper" in favor of simply being who you are and using those badass traits for good. The book covers in good detail how to resist and respond to systematic oppression of the self by viewing the topic through the lens of self-help. What we are left with is not a traditional touchy-feely self-help book, but rather a roadmap for truly badass, unapologetic, authentic living.

The book is mostly geared to readers who feel they have that spark of badass in them, but who have not taken the leap to say, "This is me." By using a conversational, feisty tone and anecdotal evidence from her own journey to self-discovery, Sincero shows us that she is one of us. Readers relate to her, because she shows that the journey to self-discovery is messy, raw, and often rife with missteps. That ethos helps the reader trust her and believe they, too, can channel their inner badass. What the book lacks, however, is anecdotal evidence outside the scope of Sincero's personal experience and a connection to a greater narrative of what it means to be "badass." It's focused on her interior world, and that's where the connection stops for the reader.

My book, however, is specifically designed to chart the broader narrative of what it means to be a badass, and show readers that they are part of a grand tradition of resistance—whether they are resisting an identity assigned to them that doesn't quite fit or a system of religious or professional oppression that is keeping them and others from living authentically. In Sister Resisters, readers will be able to connect to stories and anecdotes from women throughout history and see themselves as part of a long tradition of badass women who work to create a more equitable space for all participants of a system.

Women and Power: A Manifesto
Mary Beard (Liveright, 2017)
ISBN 978-1631494758
Amazon Sales Ranking: 13,970
Noted classicist Mary Beard delivers a powerhouse punch to the gut of misogyny in *Women and Power: A Manifesto*. Brief in length but deep in scope, this short book walks readers through the history of empirical, systematic oppression of women from the time of Homer to the age of Trump. Beard succinctly lays out the timeline of misogyny as it relates to leadership and power and draws a direct line between our cultural assumptions about women's roles in power structures and the fights we keep fighting but can't seem to win. It's a must-read for any feminist scholar.

What the book has in clear analysis, it lacks in narrative. While Beard does an excellent job of connecting these historical women to how we view power today, it lacks a rich narrative backstory for each woman. While the reader can certainly appreciate Beard's direct approach, it may leave some hungering for more story and less theory.

That's what *Sister Resisters* provides. While my book does not linger on the biographical background, it does delve into it for each woman so the reader can see an organic trajectory of her resistance work. For many of these women, the minutiae of life provided an impetus to resist, and those narrative stories are what really make each woman unique and impactful for today's reader. The goal of *Sister Resisters* is that the reader gets to know each woman's arc of resistance and can see themselves in the book. The action plan, then, is relatable, useful, and deeply personal for each reader.

My Badass Book of Saints: Courageous Women Who Showed Me How to Live
Maria Morera Johnson (Ave Maria Press, 2015)
ISBN 978-1594716324
Amazon Sales Ranking: 69,773
Catholic blogger and popular podcaster Maria Morera Johnson (*Catholic Weekend* pod) explores the lives and work of 24 religious women who portray how to live a virtuous life under often dangerous and oppressive circumstances. Johnson paints a personal narrative here, focusing on her own experience as a Cuban American Catholic woman and the religious women throughout history who have inspired her. Though the focus is not on these women's resistance work that theme shines through with stories about badass women like Sister Blandina Segale who tried (and failed) to evangelize Billy the Kid to change his ways, and Nazi resister Irena Sendler, who helped smuggle children out of the Warsaw Ghetto during World War II. Johnson's real gift is making these stories personal, and you feel her love for these women.

Though the book contains a useful group discussion guide, it is solely focused on Johnson's worldview and life experiences. Some readers will see themselves in her narrative, but the direct application to their own lives may get lost in the shuffle. Like most books with an autobiographical narrative arc, this book leaves the reader herself unaddressed and only seeing these women through the writer's personal lens.

Sister Resisters is laser-focused on the reader's experience and not about the author's connection to the subject. What I try to do for the reader is to highlight the stories of these heroic women in a way that allows the reader to see themselves in the women's experiences. What I do *not* do is write about these women in a way that suggests there is only one way to interpret them—which is, frankly, what so many of these personal books on women of faith tend to do. I want the reader to breathe in the narratives, make the connection between the resistance work of these women and themselves, and then take action to break down the barriers that hold them back in their own systems, whether in the workplace, home, religion, or political landscape.

ABOUT THE AUTHOR

Dr. Jennifer Dorsey knows a lot about two things: books and women. A 25-year veteran of the book publishing industry, she has worked for both small, indie presses and large national publishers. As an editor, she has worked with books on topics ranging from history and self-help to technology and business. She has served as a co-author and ghostwriter for 11 books in the technology, business, and medical categories (even though she's not **that** kind of doctor). She has written and presented widely about issues related to writing and feminist rhetoric, which was the focus of her doctoral work.

After realizing that following a traditional academic path wasn't her calling, she made a break from the ivory tower and decided to write what she wanted (irreverent, timely non-fiction) for whom she wanted (badass, bookish feminists). She has presented her research on rhetoric, writing, and women's studies at conferences for the Council of College Composition and Communication (3,000 attendees), Writing Program Administrators of America (1,000 attendees), Midwest Modern Language Association (1,000 attendees), Feminist Rhetorics (1,000 attendees), and the Pop Culture Association of America (3,000 attendees). Once the book is placed, she will devote more time to pursuing similar speaking opportunities and add a circuit of women's studies guest lectures at premier US universities.

She serves as a volunteer curriculum development committee member and instructor for the Saint Louis University Prison Program and sits on the board of the MICA (Migrant and Immigrant Community Action) Project for the St. Louis region, an organization that helps provide low-cost legal representation and lower barriers to justice for DREAMers and asylum seekers.

AUTHOR'S PREVIOUS PUBLICATIONS

Books (Consumer Trade)

- *Medical Terminology for Dummies, Second Edition*. John Wiley & Sons, 2015. Co-author.
- *Start a Business in Texas*, Entrepreneur Press, 2015. Revising author.
- *Start a Business in Virginia*, Entrepreneur Press, 2015. Revising author.
- *Start a Business in Washington*, Entrepreneur Press, 2015. Revising author.
- *Start a Business in California*, Entrepreneur Press, 2015. Revising author.
- *Start a Business in Florida*, Entrepreneur Press, 2015. Revising author.
- *Start a Business in New York*, Entrepreneur Press, 2015. Revising author.
- *Electronic Health Records for Dummies*. John Wiley & Sons, 2010. Co-author.
- *Green Business Practices for Dummies*, John Wiley & Sons, 2009. Ghostwriter.
- *Medical Terminology for Dummies*. John Wiley & Sons, 2008. Co-author.
- *How to Start Your Own Import/Export Business*, Second Edition. Entrepreneur Press, 2007. Revising author.
- *How to Start Your Own Medical Claims Billing Business*, Second Edition. Entrepreneur Press, 2007. Revising author

Journal Article

- *Renewing Our Commitment: A Multimodal Journey Through CCCC*. Pearson Education CompPro Professional Development Online Journal: http://www.pearsonhighered.com/cccc2010_emergingpedagogies/. 2010.

Book Chapter

- "Sites of Writing: Fanny Fern and the Space of Normativity in 19th Century Publishing" in *Feminist Challenges, Feminist Rhetorics: Locations, Scholarship, and Discourse.* Cambridge Scholars Press, April 2014.

PLATFORM AND MARKETING PLAN

Having one foot in the academic space and one in the publishing world, Dr. Dorsey will be using both avenues of her platform to build a marketing plan for Sister Resisters. Here is a look at her current platform specs:

- Personal e-mail list: 5,000
- Combined personal social (Facebook, Twitter, Instagram, LinkedIn): 1,500
- Combined affiliated e-mail lists (alumni groups, professional organizations, etc.): 50,000
- Relationships with college alumni publications with combined circulation of over 500,000
- Existing relationship with national media outlets with readership across all platforms of over 11 million.
- 3-5 speaking engagements per year at premiere academic conferences such as CCCC (3,000 attendees) and MLA (5,500 attendees).

To promote *Sister Resisters*, author will:

- Work with PR firm to build a targeted PR campaign in advance of book launch to include radio, TV, print, social, and web components.
- Dedicate budget and resources to a pre-order campaign targeting approximately 10,000 contacts derived from e-mail list, social, and alumni e-mail lists.
- Create a recurring social media blast to both personal and site/ pod-affiliated accounts.

- Secure feature article and 3-5 self-authored contributions to website/social verticals with a combined readership of over 11 million. Topics will be related to women in business and using your brand for resistance work.
- Create and send an e-mail blast campaign targeting personal list of 5,000.
- Work with alumni publications (500,000 readers) to secure articles or mentions of the book.
- Actively work to secure speaking engagements at 2019 CCCC (3,000 attendees), MLA (5,500 attendees), Midwest MLA (1,000 attendees), and Feminist Rhetorics (1,000 attendees) for 2019 with back-of-room sales and conference store book sales component.
- Aggressively pursue opportunities to be a guest on the podcasts of the authors and agents whose books I've worked with, as well as personal connections who have successful blogs. (Estimated reach: 2.35 million listeners)
- Professional website to go live in 6 months featuring blogs and articles focused on books, politics, business, and pop culture with a feminist voice. The site will be linked to corporate partner accounts and will feature an affiliate store. The website will also maintain a social media presence with related verticals on Facebook, Twitter, and Instagram highlighting top stories, live events, and platform-embedded sales for this book.
- Mouthy podcast to launch in 6 months featuring interviews on and stories with badass women resisters from all sectors, including religion, business, and political. Each episode will feature an interview with a "mouthy broad" as well as shorter featurettes like: Patriarchy Smasher of the Week, Men We Love to Piss Off, Your Feminist Agenda (to-do list for social/political action items for listeners), and Amplify This (giving shout outs to women who are doing something amazing and could use a PR boost). We are currently seeking lateral relationships with other feminist-centric pods for cross-marketing, including *Hysteria*, *Book Squad Goals*, *Call Your Girlfriend*, and *The History Chicks*.

Need Additional Support?

I'M HERE FOR YOU.

I created the **Write Your Book Proposal Course** in partnership with Broad Book Group to help you harness the power of authorship as a unique leverage for your business growth.

This course is self-paced where I help you develop a strategic asset that elevates your brand, engages your perfect client, and positions you as an authority in your field with video tutorials and worksheets.

You can take the course in tandem while you read this book, or watch a video module to help you dig into a specific part of the process. Think of it like having a one-on-one coaching session with me at any time of day.

Ready? Scan the QR code or visit:

broadbookgroup.com/winning-book-proposal-course

Printed in the USA
CPSIA information can be obtained
at www.ICGtesting.com
JSHW070509160624
64895JS00004B/4

9 798985 191332